The Hearts Story

An Official History of
Heart of Midlothian
Football Club

Roddy Mackenzie

g

Grange
Lomond Books

© 1998
Published by Grange Communications Ltd
Edinburgh

Printed in the UK

ISBN 0 947782 11 7

Contents

ROOTS

FOOTBALL was still finding its feet when Heart of Midlothian came into being. The rules of the game were still being formulated and, until the latter half of the nineteenth century, different rules were adhered to in different areas. It was not until carrying the ball and hacking were outlawed that the game became recognisable as what it is today.

The Football Association in England was formed in 1863 and it was Queen's Park, who had played in the first FA Cup, who led the move for a Scottish association to be formed in 1873, around the same time as Hearts were born.

There are conflicting stories on how Hearts originated in 1873-74. The most favoured explanation is that the team was founded by youngsters who played football on the site of the old Edinburgh Tolbooth jail in the Royal Mile which was nicknamed the 'Heart of Midlothian' after Walter Scott's novel and which closed in 1817. To mark the site, a Heart of Midlothian was set in the cobblestones which is still there today. The story goes that the local authorities were unhappy at youngsters playing on the site which had seen many public hangings and told them to play on the Meadows. Another story which also has support is that the team was named after a local dancehall which the youngsters used to frequent until a local police constable suggested they would be better off kicking a football and forming a team. Hearts' first captain, Tom Purdie, is also given credit for naming the team *'Heart of Midlothian'*. He won the captaincy after a one-on-one game with another leading player at the time, Jake Reid, who, it is said, put through his own goal, which effectively handed Purdie the captaincy.

Hearts played their first matches at the Meadows, and, after a short time at Powburn, later moved to Powderhall and then to Old Tynecastle in 1881, which was across the road from the current ground, in which Hearts finally took up residence in 1886. Only in the most recent years, has a move out of Tynecastle been contemplated but the ground has now been refurbished to accommodate the club into the next century.

Hearts' original colours were red, white and blue but, as early as 1878, maroon was adopted. According to one historian, maroon was the colour worn by St Andrew's FC, which also played at the Meadows and, when Hearts disbanded for a time, some players joined St Andrew and the teams effectively merged. Football was becoming more established in Edinburgh due to a keen rivalry with Hibernian, a club set up by Irish immigrants. The first meeting of the clubs in 1875 resulted in a 3-1 win for Hearts and the rivalry between the clubs has never waned since.

On October 30, 1880, Hearts recorded what was their biggest confirmed victory when they beat Anchor 21-0 in the Edinburgh FA Cup. Elsewhere, five years later, on September 5, 1885, Arbroath beat Bon Accord 36-0 in the first round of the Scottish Cup, still a record scoreline for an official match. Not so well known is that, on the same day, Dundee Harp beat Aberdeen Rovers 35-0.

In the early days of Scottish football, professionalism was frowned upon. In 1884, the Scottish Football Association (SFA) suspended 57 Scottish players who had gone south of the border to play for English professional teams, ten of which were former Hearts players, who were banned from ever playing in Scotland again. In 1885-86, professional football was permitted in England and Hearts (along with Rangers, Queen's Park, Partick Thistle and Third Lanark) entered the English FA Cup. Hearts later scratched for fear of punishment from the SFA. The following year Hearts took up their FA Cup place, only to lose in the opening round to Darwen

7-1 but then the SFA introduced a rule that none of its member clubs could play in another association's national competition.

In September 1887, Hearts beat Vale of Midlothian 18-0 at Tynecastle in the first round of the Edinburgh Shield, even though they were four players short of their best team. As the *Edinburgh Evening News* reported: *"The resistance offered at the outset was of a passable nature but after half an hour had gone, there were but feeble attempts made by the visitors."*

Hearts were at the sharp end of the new laws and in 1890-91, the club was responsible for the inauguration of the penalty kick when one of their fullbacks, Jimmy Adams, punched the ball out of the goal in a Scottish Cup tie against East Stirlingshire in Falkirk. The incident provoked fans to riot and the SFA decided that there must be a more stringent punishment than a free-kick when a player prevents a certain goal in this manner.

Hearts, incidentally, took it all in their stride as they went on to defeat Third Lanark at Cathkin and then Dumbarton 1-0 in the final at Ibrox, when Willie Mason scored the only goal. Five years later, Hearts won the cup again, this time in the only final ever played in Edinburgh, when they edged out Hibs by 3-1 at Logie Green.

Before a crowd of 16,034, Hearts had three survivors from the 1891 cup-winning team - Isaac Begbie, David Russell and David Baird. According to Albert Mackie *('The Hearts')*, Hearts had a forward line which *"coruscated with ingenuity and enterprise"* and their goals came from Baird (penalty), Alex King and Willie Michael.

Hearts, the only club from the East of Scotland, were one of the founder members of the Scottish League in 1890 along with Rangers, Renton, Abercorn, Dumbarton, Cowlairs, Cambuslang, Celtic, St Mirren, Third Lanark and Vale of Leven.

Hearts lost 5-2 to Rangers at Ibrox in their first league match on August 18, 1890, after which the *Edinburgh Evening News* wrote: *"such a result as a victory for the Glasgow team by five goal to two was never dreamed of, far less anticipated."*

The first home game was against Celtic at Tynecastle and resulted in a 5-0 defeat, which prompted the *Evening News* to say: *"such players as MacPherson, Begbie, Hill, Mason and Mackay seem, for the time being, to have lost the ability which gained them fame."*

Before the season kicked off, Hearts were, according to local reports, in need of a capable centre. If modern-day players feel they are over-scrutinised at times, then the reporter on the *Edinburgh Evening News* did not pull his punches as he pinpointed the weakness. He wrote: *"Wilson is by no means class enough, the work would be too arduous for Jenkinson and, in the absence of any junior with good credentials, there seems no alternative but to leave the district in the search for a suitable player."*

An example of how football was becoming increasingly popular, is backed up by scrutiny of the personal advertising columns of the *Edinburgh Evening News* on August 14, 1890, which read: *"Footballer (stranger to Edinburgh) wishes to join good club. Good back or halfback."*

Hearts won the League Championship for the first time in 1895, when they lost only two of their 18 matches and scored 50 goals in the process. Two years later, the title was recaptured after Hibs had set the early pace in the Championship. But, at the start of the season, Hearts had made a significant signing in Bobby Walker, who was destined to become the first 'superstar' of the club. Hearts had to beat Clyde 'home' and 'away' to win the title in 1897 and they did so 5-1 and 5-0 and, with Celtic losing to Dundee, Hearts won the title with two points to spare.

While it was the last league title Hearts were to win for 61 years, this was truly a golden era for the club and the Scottish Cup was won for the third time in 1901 with a thrilling 4-3 final win over Celtic at Hampden. Mark Bell (2), Bobby Walker and Charlie Thomson scored the goals. Five years later, Hearts won the cup again, this time with a 1-0 win over Third Lanark, with George Wilson scoring the only goal of the game.

Under manager John McCartney, Hearts had what was widely held to be one of the best teams in their history (Boyd; Crossan and Carrie; Briggs, Mercer and Nellies; Low, Wattie, Gracie, Graham and Wilson). But the team was torn apart by the First World War. The Hearts players had set an example by all enlisting in Sir George McCrae's Battalion, the 16th Royal Scots.

Unfortunately, seven of the squad paid the ultimate price and were killed in action or on service: Duncan Currie, Tom Gracie, Harry Wattie, James Speedie, Tom Allan, Archie Boyd and Ernest Ellis. Furthermore, Bob Mercer and Paddy Crossan were among those wounded or gassed, while Mercer never played league football again and died on a football field in 1926.

A War Memorial was built at Haymarket at the west end of Edinburgh in 1922 to players and members of the club who lost their lives in the war and current Hearts players and officials attend the annual Remembrance Day service at the monument every November.

Understandably, it was not easy for Hearts to recover from such a heavy toll of casualties from the war. In the twenties, their highest-placed league finish was third and it was not until 1956 that another Scottish Cup final was reached. But Hearts still managed to produce players of top quality, one being Barney Battles who scored 44 league goals in 1930-31, which is still a record. In 1932, Hearts played in front of their record Tynecastle crowd, when 53,396 fans turned up to see a Scottish Cup match which Rangers won 1-0.

On September 21, 1935, Hearts beat Hibs 8-2 to record their biggest league win over their oldest rivals and less than two years later, when Hearts beat Stirling's King's Park 15-0 in the second round of the Scottish Cup on February 13, 1937, Willie Walsh scored eight goals.

Austria's Rapid Vienna were the first foreign team to play at Tynecastle in August, 1934, when Hearts won an exhibition match 5-1 and Iceland's Otto Jonsson became Tynecastle's first foreign import when he played in 1943-44.

It was during the thirties that Tommy Walker came to prominence. He made a big impact on the team and also graced the Scotland team, where he scored a famous penalty against England at Wembley after the ball had rolled off the spot three times. He was the most talented inside-forward of his generation and was a true sportsman, which won him many admirers. Hearts finished runners-up to Celtic for the league in 1938 but then the Second World War intervened. However, it was in the years immediately after the war that Hearts' most successful side was fashioned.

HOME IMPROVEMENT

HEARTS moved into their present ground at Tynecastle in 1886 when a new grandstand was constructed at a cost of £200. Hearts' final match at Old Tynecastle was on February 27, 1886, when a 2,000 crowd saw them defeat Sunderland 2-1. Hearts turned to English opposition again to formally open the new ground on April 4, with Bolton Wanderers providing the opposition this time. Between 5,000-6,000 turned out to watch the game and again it resulted in a victory - 4-1 on this occasion, with Tommy Jenkinson, Hearts' first Scotland international cap, gaining the distinction of scoring the first goal at the new ground.

Two years afterwards, as the popularity of the team grew, two new stands and a pavilion were built on the east side of the stadium which took the capacity up to 10,000. In 1892, the first covered accommodation was offered to spectators when a roof was added to the south-east stand and refreshment kiosks were introduced two years later. Tynecastle was taking shape and another covered stand - this time replacing the north-east stand - was constructed in 1901 and the banking around the pitch was extended to take the capacity up to 20,000, a figure Hearts reached in a Scottish Cup semi final with Hibs that year.

With crowds flocking to the ground, the stadium developed quickly. The north and south stands were combined in 1903 and the bankings were extended further three years later and a cycle track around the pitch removed, which took the capacity of Tynecastle above 60,000. By the end of 1911, a covered enclosure with a capacity of 4,500 was added which became known as the 'Iron Stand'.

The present main stand was built in 1914 at a cost of £12,178 and, in 1925, the club purchased the ground from Edinburgh Corporation at a cost of £5,000 but there was a 'buy-back' clause in the agreement which was not bought out by the club until 1977. In 1926, Hearts started further redevelopment work at a cost of £18,000. A new entrance was built at Wheatfield Street and terracing around the ground was added and banked with the help of old railway sleepers. The 'Iron Stand' was demolished to make way for the terracing and the capacity of the ground by 1930 was 55,842. The ground saw its record attendance two years later when Rangers visited for a Scottish Cup tie on February 13 1932 and a crowd of 53,396 looked on.

During the Second World War, attendances at matches were restricted to 8,000 due to the threat of air raids but police discretion could lead to this figure, on occasion, being higher.

After the war, the terracing was concreted and certain essential safety work implemented and, although the capacity of the ground was now 54,359, a limit of 49,000 was set for safety reasons. Floodlights were installed in 1957 at a cost of £14,000 and two years later a further £23,000 was spent on a covered enclosure to hold 15,000 spectators. Security fences and segregation barriers were erected in 1978 to comply with safety regulations and work on corporate hospitality boxes was done in 1984 as Hearts sought to increase revenue through their growing commercial backing.

That year also saw the floodlighting upgraded to European standard and, the following year, a family enclosure with seating for 1,000 was opened as the club became increasingly aware of attracting a new generation of supporters.

Major decisions had to be taken in light of the Taylor Report following the Hillsborough tragedy in 1989 and Hearts looked set to leave Tynecastle and the club canvassed supporters for their opinions. The club looked at 14 possible sites throughout Lothian Region and the then chairman, Wallace Mercer, was content to explore all of the options and urged, *"I don't think we should suddenly make the most momentous decision that may have influenced Hearts since its inception without pulling together all the facts."*

Hearts considered a ground-sharing option with Hibs at an out-of-town site which seemed a logical alternative with both clubs having trouble raising the necessary finance to bring their respective grounds up to scratch. But no agreement was reached and it looked likely that Hearts would move to Millerhill, on the south-east outskirts of the city, where ambitious plans were put in place for full back-up facilities. However, planning permission was not forthcoming for what was a green-belt site and Hearts were resigned to remaining at Tynecastle.

In 1993, Mercer revealed plans to buy the stadium for £2.7 million, refurbish it and then lease it back to the club on a 50-year agreement but, under pressure from shareholders and supporters, he had a re-think and a '500 Club' was set in place - whereby supporters contributed £500 each - to allow work to begin on a new 13,000-seat Wheatfield Stand. It was opened in 1994 and the following year the school-end stand was added.

The new stands brought a new atmosphere to the ground, particularly as supporters were closer to the action and it made Tynecastle a more intimidating place for visiting teams. A share scheme in 1994 had failed to raise the funds Hearts had hoped for and the club had to wait another two years to construct the Gorgie Road stand, after new revenue had been brought in through placing the club on the stock exchange. The work has brought the stadium capacity up to 18,000 and transformed the ground from what it was in the early nineties. New corporate entertainment facilites have been added and a Hearts superstore has opened. Hearts have also refurbished their office accommodation.

The next stage is to replace the main stand - built in 1914 - and Hearts are actively looking at ways that can be achieved to give the club a state-of-the-art ground early in the new century.

THE BOYS IN MAROON

The Last Line–Goalkeepers

HEARTS have produced - and attracted - goalkeepers of the highest calibre through the years. From Jock Fairbairn, who was the first Hearts goalkeeper to get his hands on silverware back in 1891, to current custodian, Gilles Rousset, who clutched the same piece of silver last May, the last line of defence has been held with distinction.

Fairbairn, one of the club's original professional players and signed in 1890 from Dalry Albert Juniors, kept a clean sheet in that first Scottish Cup Final success - a 1-0 win over Dumbarton and, after adding a League Championship medal with the club in 1895, he was back in the final in 1896, when Hearts faced Hibernian at Logie Green and helped them to a 3-1 win.

Fairbairn, the first Hearts goalkeeper to play 100 league matches and who was capped for the Scottish League, gained another League Championship medal in 1897, when Hearts won the league by just two points from Hibs.

Fairbairn left Hearts in 1899 after 281 games for the club.

Harry Rennie took over from Fairbairn but did not have the same degree of success at club level. A former halfback, he was signed from Morton and was highly regarded. He was the first Hearts goalkeeper to be capped for Scotland in 1900 but he was allowed to leave the club after Hearts did not agree to his wage demands and he joined Hibs. Before his career ended, he had won 13 caps for Scotland.

He was away from Tynecastle by the time Hearts were next in the Scottish Cup Final in 1901 and it was George Philip who stood between the posts for that occasion against Celtic in what was to prove an epic final.

Hearts, inspired by Bobby Walker, eventually won 4-3 to record their third Scottish Cup win and, in 1906, they made it four when Philip this time kept a clean sheet as Hearts beat Third Lanark 1-0 at Hampden.

Hearts also made the final in 1903, when they lost to Rangers 2-0 after two drawn matches but it was the Arbroath-born George McWattie who kept goal on those occasions. An amateur who was signed in 1901 from Queen's Park, where he had been capped twice by Scotland, McWattie made 126 appearances for the club and had 40 shut-outs.

Hearts were back at Hampden in 1907 but this time it was Tom Allan, signed from Rutherglen Glencairn, who was in goal as they lost to Celtic 3-0 in the final. Allan was transferred to Sunderland in 1908 after a dispute over wages, but returned three years later and, during the 1913-14 season, had a record 19 shut-outs in the league.

In the 1920s, Hearts paid £750 to sign Willie White from Hamilton and he proved a capable enough goalkeeper to be capped at League international level. Later in the decade, Hearts loaned goalkeeper Jock Gilfillan to East Fife and he went on to play in the 1927 Scottish Cup Final, when East Fife went down 3-1 to Celtic.

Jack Harkness was to become Hearts' most-capped goalkeeper when he collected a dozen caps - eight of which were earned when he was at Tynecastle. He played in the famous 1928 'Wembley Wizards' 5-1 win over England at Wembley. Born in Glasgow, Harkness started out with Queen's Park and won his first international cap against England in 1927 while still an amateur. He signed for Hearts just a few weeks after the 5-1 thrashing of England and played over 400 matches for the club before retiring in 1936 after being troubled by a leg injury.

One of the most popular Hearts goalkeepers down through the years was Jimmy Brown, who signed from Bayview Youth Club in 1942. He had a flamboyant personality and was a capable and agile goalkeeper who was first choice throughout the immediate post-war years. He caught the eye with his colourful tops and caps and he played in the early years of the *'Terrible Trio'*. He was also unfortunate not to win a Scottish Cup winners' medal with Hearts in 1952, when he was in the team that lost 3-1 to Motherwell in the second replay of the final. He was succeeded by Jimmy Watters who kept goal for the next two seasons before being replaced by Willie Duff.

Duff was to be the first Hearts goalkeeper to get his hands on a winner's medal of any significant description since 1906, when he played in the team that beat Motherwell 4-2 in the 1954 League Cup Final and he richly deserved it, with a commanding display which included a notable save from Willie Hunter when Hearts were under the cosh. Duff was to win another medal - this time in the Scottish Cup - in 1956 where he was last line of defence in the team that so famously beat Celtic 3-1. Duff did not concede a goal en route to the final and even Rangers were dismantled 4-0 in the quarter finals. The only goal he conceded was in the 53rd minute of the final, when he was jostled by Celtic's goalscorer, Michael Haughney, and could not hold the ball. But Duff was to leave the club later that year to do his National Service in London, where he signed for Charlton Athletic.

Wilson Brown took over in goal but his place was soon to be taken by teenager Gordon Marshall, who had signed from Dalkeith Thistle. Born in England, he was capped at Under-23 level for England, although he spent most of his time in Edinburgh. Uniquely, he was to play in three League Cup-winning teams while at Tynecastle and also in two League Championship-winning teams. Hearts only conceded 29 goals during their 1958 Championship success, when the team scored a record 132 goals and he was to be the club's first-choice goalkeeper through to the end of the 1962-63 season. Marshall, of course, was the first Hearts goalkeeper to play in Europe, when he kept goal against Standard Liege in the European Cup in 1958 and proved to be a great servant to the club. Like two other Hearts goalkeepers, Harry Rennie and Willie Waugh, he was also to have a spell at rivals Hibs.

Like Harkness, Jim Cruickshank started out his career at Queen's Park and he went on to become arguably Hearts' best-ever goalkeeper. A former Scottish Schoolboys' long jump champion, Cruickshank joined Hearts in 1960 as a teenager. He stayed at the club for 17 years and played 610 games - a total only Henry Smith has bettered as a goalkeeper for Hearts - and gained six full caps for Scotland. Sadly, his time at Hearts coincided with the lean years and, although he played in the Scottish Cup Finals of 1968 and 1976, there was to be no winner's medal to mark his career. At 5'10", he was not the tallest goalkeeper but he had great agility and kept a clean sheet in 102 of his 394 league games, which was a considerable record given Hearts' modest fortunes during his time at the club.

Within four years of Cruickshank leaving, the then Hearts manager, Tony Ford, paid Leeds United just £2,000 to bring the little-known Henry Smith to Tynecastle. Although born in Lanarkshire, he had moved to Yorkshire at an early age and had played non-league football before working down the pits. He played understudy at Leeds to David Harvey, David Stewart, John Lukic and David Seaman, before signing for Hearts in August, 1981. Smith was an ever-present and went on to overtake Cruickshank's league shut-out record and, after 15 years at the club, he recorded

Cruickshank saves Hearts again.

171 clean sheets. Like Cruickshank, he had to endure some hard years at the club but the form which took Hearts to the verge of honours won him international recognition and he represented Scotland on three occasions. Nicky Walker also had a useful spell for Hearts when Smith lost his place under Joe Jordan and he went on to gain an international cap against Germany during his time at Tynecastle.

But when Jim Jefferies arrived at Hearts, it was clear that signing a goalkeeper was one of his priorities. Smith, Craig Nelson and Gary O'Connor were all given their chance before the manager signed former French international goalkeeper, Gilles Rousset, who had played at Sochaux, Rennes, Lyon and Marseille. At 6'5" and with such a pedigree, it was scarcely believable that Jefferies could get such a player for free and he struck up an instant rapport with the Tynecastle support. A tremendous shot-stopper as well as a goalkeeper who could command his area, he gave Jefferies a solid foundation on which to build a team. The only blip in his time at Tynecastle was an uncharacteristic error in the 1996 Scottish Cup Final against Rangers but he made up for it in 1998 when he took the 'Man of the Match' award in Hearts' Cup Final win.

Edinburgh Rock–The Defence

David Weir is the latest in a long line of Hearts defenders who have played at the highest level. He vaulted into the Scotland team at France '98 after no more than a handful of friendly matches and will surely be a cornerstone of the international team in the future.

But Weir was just following the Tynecastle lineage which can be traced to the origins of the club. The first Hearts' captain, Tom Purdie, was a defender of great stature and it is even suggested in some club histories that he was the man who first thought of the name *'Heart of*

Midlothian'. He certainly took his captaincy seriously and it is said that when Hearts beat Hibs for the President's Cup in 1878 after five hard-fought draws, he beat off an irate group of Hibs' supporters with a cabby's whip when they tried to attack the cab the players had hired to parade the trophy through the city.

Hearts also had a fullback, Nick Ross, in those early days, who was widely regarded as the best defender of his generation. He was ahead of his time and is believed to have introduced the pass back to the goalkeeper which soon spread throughout the game. However, the lure of the professional game in England became too much to resist and Ross soon joined Preston North End. When Hearts won the Scottish Cup with a memorable 4-3 win over Celtic at Ibrox and the great Bobby Walker stole the show, they also had the charismatic Albert Buick at the heart of their defence and his energetic style won him a lot of admirers before he, too, moved to England.

Charlie Thomson, originally a centre-forward, was converted to centre-half and he was rated one of the best in Britain. He played in the 1901 final and captained the Hearts team that won the trophy again in 1906 and, in all, won 21 international caps for Scotland, a dozen of which were awarded while at Tynecastle. He joined Sunderland for the then maximum transfer fee of £350 in 1909. As the First World War approached, Hearts possessed what was widely believed to be one of their best ever teams. One of the most outstanding players was fullback, Paddy Crossan, who played almost 400 matches for the club. He was one of the 16 players who volunteered to fight for his country in 1914 and he went on to play for the club until 1925. Centre-half, Bob Mercer, was another who fought in the war and he returned in poor health after being gassed. He collapsed on the football field during a benefit match at Selkirk and died at the age of just 37 from a heart attack.

In the thirties, Hearts also had a imposing centre-half of some note in John Johnstone, who was to gain three full international caps for Scotland and replaced veteran Alex Wright in the Tynecastle team. He played over 300 times for the club before joining Arbroath in 1935 for a £5,000 fee. At right-back in the thirties was Andy Anderson, who made his international debut for Scotland against England at the age of 24. He played over 450 times for Hearts and is the club's second most-capped player, with 23 appearances for his country.

Another fullback who gave great service to the club in the thirties and forties was Duncan McClure who was with the club for 15 years and played over 400 matches. He gained a wartime cap against England in 1940 and retired from the game eight years later. Bobby Dougan made a name for himself as a dominant centre-back in the late forties and early fifties after converting from halfback. He gained one full cap for Scotland before joining Kilmarnock in 1954.

As Hearts approached their most successful spell in their history, they had a defence that took the strain when the prolific forward line was finding the going tough. Bobby Parker, who was to go on and serve the club as a director and as chairman, signed in 1947 and, playing mainly at right-back, captained the team between 1949-56. He captained the team to the historic League Cup win in 1954 - the first major honour since 1906 - but missed the 1956 Scottish Cup Final win due to a cartilage injury. He served the club as player, coach, scout and director for 45 years and was hugely popular. It was Freddie Glidden, brought up in Lanarkshire and who played for Whitburn Juniors and Newtongrange Star before joining Hearts, who captained the Hearts team in the 1956 final. He started as a right-back but became outstanding at centre-half and never was he more popular than the evening he brought the Scottish Cup back to Edinburgh.

Another very consistent fullback of the fifties and early sixties was Bobby Kirk. Signed from Raith Rovers in 1955, he went on to win two League Championship medals, two League Cup medals and a Scottish Cup medal with Hearts. He played 365 games for the club and scored 12 goals from the penalty spot. Davie Holt was another solid fullback for Hearts and policed the left side of defence for Hearts for 350 games. He also won five caps for Scotland but was not noted for his attacking qualities. During his time at Tynecastle he never scored a goal!

Dave Clunie, Arthur Mann, Roy Kay, Andy Lynch and a certain Jim Jefferies all filled the fullback roles with distinction in the sixties and seventies, as Hearts sought to recapture the glory days. None managed to win a Scotland cap but all made a big contribution to the club. Jefferies never gave less than a hundred per cent and was an example to those around him with his leadership qualities. Strong in the tackle and a player who read the game perceptively, he was a great asset to the club. Another popular 'stopper' was Alan Anderson who was the kingpin of the Tynecastle defence at the time. The imposing centre-half went on to play 537 games, over 350 in the league, after signing in 1962 from Scunthorpe. He was also a useful weapon at set-pieces, such was his power in the air. Eddie Thomson, later to become manager of Australia, was a well-respected figure at Tynecastle and also had a spell as captain.

During the troubled times of the late seventies/early eighties, Walter Kidd emerged as a right-back of great endeavour. He captained the club to promotion in 1983 and also to the verge of the league title three years later. A player of great commitment, his only blemish was being sent off in the 1986 Scottish Cup Final against Aberdeen. One of the most cultured defenders to wear maroon was Craig Levein, signed at a bargain.price from Cowdenbeath by Alex MacDonald. He went on to play 16 times for his country but serious knee injuries forced him out of the game. He is now making a name for himself in management but will always be highly thought of at Tynecastle. Dave McPherson is another established Scotland international defender who has given great service to Hearts during two spells. He gained every domestic honour in the game with Rangers and battled back from injury to help Hearts lift the 1998 Scottish Cup.

Alan McLaren was mature beyond his years when he burst into the Hearts team and it was only a matter of time before he moved to Rangers for £1.25 million in a deal which saw McPherson returning to Tynecastle. McLaren, as predicted by manager MacDonald when he played his first match for Hearts, went on to establish himself in the international team but 24 caps was a paltry return for a player of such promise and his career also ended prematurely due to injury.

There is no doubt he was helped in his development by Sandy Jardine, who joined Hearts after an illustrious career with Rangers and Scotland but still had a lot to offer. Both Levein and McLaren benefited from his background and he eased their passage into the Premier Division.

Hearts have continued to rear solid defenders. Paul Ritchie had an outstanding season in 1997-98 and is on the verge of full international honours. He has shown maturity and vision far beyond his years and has played at every level for his country apart from senior level. He has formed a formidable partnership with David Weir, who shows a calm head and excellent distribution and his ability to anticipate what the opposition will do is a strength that has won him a place on the international stage.

One defender who has epitomised the new Hearts is Gary Locke. Named as a substitute on the last day of the 1992-93 season against St Johnstone as a 17-year-old, Locke quickly matured into a top-class defender.

His unquestionable dedication (he has supported the club for as long as he can remember) has made him an invaluable asset and Jim Jefferies was quick to acknowledge his contribution when he named him as captain at the age of 20. Locke is tigerish in the tackle, has boundless energy and is equally effective in midfield, where his future may lie.

Unfortunate to have been injured after eight minutes of the 1996 Scottish Cup Final against Rangers, he also missed the League Cup Final the following season and the 1998 Scottish Cup Final win due to injuries. But there are clearly going to be more opportunities for him to secure that elusive winner's medal.

Gary Naysmith is also fast making a name for himself, not just with his defensive talents but his forays forward and his explosive shot, which has brought some spectacular goals. Grant Murray and Dave Murie also look bright prospects for the future.

The Engine Room–The Midfield

It is often referred to as the 'engine room' of a team; the midfield or, in past years, the half-back line has served to provide the forwards with the ammunition to shoot the opposition down.

One of the first midfield players to make a mark for Hearts was Isaac Begbie, who played over 400 games for the club at the end of the 19th century. He stood just 5'8" but could handle himself in the thick of midfield. He played in Hearts' Scottish Cup-winning teams of 1891 and 1896 and also the Championship-winning teams of 1895 and 1897. He also scored in Hearts' first-ever league match against Rangers in 1890.

Another diminutive midfield player around this time was George Key, who stood only 5'4". He was a firm favourite with the fans and played in the 1901 Scottish Cup Final victory over Celtic. He played less than a hundred matches for the club before moving south to Chelsea but was capped by Scotland.

Also at the turn of the century, George Hogg was earning plaudits as a defensive halfback. He captained the team in the 1896 Scottish Cup Final and also played in the 1901 final. He played twice for Scotland - against England and Ireland - before emigrating to South Africa.

Peter Nellies was a halfback of note in the early part of the 20th century and was in the side that many believed was the greatest in the history of the club in 1914. Nellies was capped twice for Scotland.

Alex Massie was signed by Willie McFarlane from Bury as an inside-forward in 1930. By converting him to right-half, McFarlane found he had bought one of the most effective players in the history of the club. He was capped 14 times for Scotland in that position and captained his country on most of those occasions. He was transferred in 1935 to Aston Villa, a club where he later became manager.

John Cumming signed for Hearts in 1950 and was to be associated with the club until 1976.

An inspirational figure who started out as a winger, Cumming found his true position as a defensive left-half. A fitness fanatic, he won every domestic honour in the game with Hearts, including four League Cup medals and captained the team to the 1962 League Cup triumph over Kilmarnock. John played 613 matches for Hearts and was capped nine times for Scotland between 1955-60. He became trainer of the club in 1967.

One of the greatest players in Hearts' history - and one of the best Scotland has produced - is Dave Mackay. Any player from Hearts' golden era of the late fifties will tell you how much they owed to Mackay before he left to join Bill Nicholson's Tottenham Hotspur for a fee of £32,000 in 1959. A tough, uncompromising player, Mackay was the driving force behind the team that ended the long trophy famine with the League Cup in 1954. He captained the side to the League Championship in 1958 and went on to play 22 times for Scotland. He was no less an influence at Tottenham, where he helped them to the English League and Cup 'double' in 1961-62, making 'Spurs' the first team in the 20th century to achieve the feat that many had believed impossible. He also helped turn unfashionable Derby into English champions in 1972.

Willie Hamilton was a different type of midfield player but, if not quite so awesome to play against, incredibly gifted. Signed in 1962 from Middlesbrough, within a matter of months he was the star of the show in the 1962 League Cup Final win over Kilmarnock. Willie was transferred to Hibs, where he became a full international and also had a spell at Aston Villa before returning to Hearts to finish his Scottish career.

Jim Brown and Ralph Callachan were two midfield players who sampled life at both Hearts and Hibs and who were both firm favourites with the Tynecastle support. Both played in the 1976 Scottish Cup Final defeat by Rangers at Hampden. Brown, who also played at fullback, turned professional when he left school at 17 and was a mainstay of the club for a decade. His career ended prematurely through injury. Callachan was a creative player who had undoubted potential but Hearts allowed him to be sold to Newcastle for £90,000, a move which was not met with approval by supporters.

Similarly, Eamonn Bannon was thought to be one of the most promising youngsters on Hearts' books and he quickly lived up to his billing. His talents complemented the industry of Cammy Fraser in midfield and, at least in the fans' eyes, his elevation to the first team had eased the pain of losing Callachan two years earlier. But, with the club facing difficult financial times, Bannon was sold to Chelsea for £215,000 and it was a move that caused a storm of protest. Bannon was to return late in his career, where he still had plenty to offer after playing eleven times for Scotland.

Gary Mackay was a midfield player who had maroon in his blood. He attended Tynecastle High School and was part of the re-emergence of the club in the eighties. Signed by Bobby Moncur, he made his Hearts debut at the age of 16 and his linking play with another youngster, John Robertson, which bordered on the telepathic, was a feature of Hearts throughout the eighties. Having played under Andy Roxburgh for the Scotland youth side, he went on to win four full Scottish caps. The most memorable was his debut against Bulgaria in Sofia in 1987, when he scored a superb winning goal in the closing minutes - a win that put the Republic of Ireland into the 1988 European Championship finals at Bulgaria's expense. Mackay played a record 515

Gary Mackay celebrates another goal.

league matches for Hearts (737 in all competitions), a total that is unlikely to be surpassed. His allegiance to the club is such that, even after signing for Airdrie, he still watches Hearts at every opportunity and shared in the 1998 Scottish Cup success from the stands.

Mackay was nurtured through those early days by Alex MacDonald, later to become manager of the club. His arrival from Rangers was significant, as he gave Hearts some much-needed guidance both on and off the field at the time. As in his Ibrox days, he had an eye for a goal and his enthusiasm for the game rubbed off on those around him.

Midfield remains the key area of a team and Hearts possess some mobile players in that department. Colin Cameron has been a revelation since signing from Raith Rovers and his late runs into opposing penalty areas have brought Hearts goals aplenty. There is no doubt Hearts miss him when he is absent through injury and his boundless energy makes him virtually impossible to mark out of a game.

Steve Fulton is also fulfilling the potential of his early days at Celtic. There were some eyebrows raised when Jim Jefferies brought him from Brockville but his use of the ball and high workrate meant he was perhaps the key player for Hearts in the successful 1997-98 campaign. Steve also enjoys getting on the scoresheet and it was no surprise that he was made captain for the Scottish Cup Final against Rangers, with Gary Locke out through injury.

Italian, Stefano Salvatori has played the holding role in midfield and, having played at the highest level in 'Serie A', is an influential player. He covers every blade of turf during a match and his great strength is closing players down and reducing their influence on a match. Salvatori rarely plays a careless pass and has been a big hit with Hearts.

The technically gifted Thomas Flogel can operate in midfield or attack. The Austrian international quickly settled into the pace of the Scottish game and is now a valuable member of the first-team squad, where he presents different options for Jim Jefferies.

Forward Thinkers–The Attack

Since the early days, Hearts have been blessed with forwards who have been admired throughout Scotland, sometimes throughout Europe and occasionally throughout the world. Bobby Walker, Tommy Walker, Willie Bauld and John Robertson can cut a line through the 20th century. Bobby Walker and John Robertson were the bookends of the century. Walker, rated as the outstanding player of his generation, starred in Hearts' 1901 Scottish Cup-winning team and Robertson was finally a cup winner in the penultimate year of the century.

Tommy Jenkinson was one of the first Hearts forwards to get amongst the goals. A strong, direct winger, he had the distinction of scoring the first goal at Tynecastle when he found the net in a 4-1 win over Bolton Wanderers in an exhibition match on April 10, 1886. A year later, he won a Scotland cap against Northern Ireland - the first Hearts player to gain international recognition.

One of the most prolific scorers at the end of the 19th century was David Baird, who scored almost 200 goals for the club and played in 450 games. He is the only Hearts player to have appeared in three Scottish Cup-winning teams and he also won three Scotland caps between 1890-92. Willie Michael was another with an eye for a goal and once scored in ten successive matches for the club but moved to Bristol City in 1900. There was also Alex Menzies, who was the first Hearts player to score 20 league goals in a season - something he managed in 1905-06.

But it was Bobby Walker, who joined Hearts in 1896, who first put the club on the map. Having come to prominence with Dalry Primrose, he was one of the most admired inside-forwards in Europe. He had a deceptive style but had a masterly touch on the ball and was admired wherever he played. Even King Haakon of Norway came to see him play during Hearts' Scandinavian tour of 1912, such had his fame spread. The 1901 final was named 'The Walker Final', such was the influence he had on the outcome of the game and he was Scotland's most-capped player at the time. With 29 caps spanning 1900-13, he remains the club's most-capped player. He played eleven times for Scotland against England and was the first Hearts player to score 100 league goals. His contribution to the growth of the club cannot be overstated.

If Walker was the architect, then Percy Dawson was more than willing to supply the finished product. The Englishman hit an astonishing 99 goals in 117 competitive matches for Hearts between 1911-14 before he signed for Blackburn Rovers for a then record fee of £2,500.

Another prolific scorer was Jock White, whose two brothers, Willie and Tom, also played for Hearts at some stage. In his first season with Hearts, Jock was leading scorer with 29 goals in 1922-23 and he went on to net 217 goals in 370 games. One hundred and fifty-four of those were in the league, a figure only four Hearts players have since bettered. Barney Battles is another forward who has a special place in Tynecastle history. Son of Barney senior, who also played with Hearts, he scored 44 league goals in season 1930-31 - a record which will surely stand the test of time. Capped once by America where he grew up, he had great ability in the air and many goals came from his head.

Dave McCulloch proved one of Hearts' most prolific scorers. He was at the club for just over a year from 1934-35 and managed to bag 55 goals in 53 league matches. Following in his footsteps, Andy Black was noted for his spectacular strikes and managed a healthy 124 league goals for Hearts before war service took him to England.

A true Tynecastle great was Tommy Walker, who was admired not just for his superb football ability but for his sporting play. Destined to become Hearts' most successful manager, he was awarded an OBE in 1960. It was clear from an early age that he had star quality. He was capped by Scotland at the age of just 19 in a match against Wales. He went on to play 20 times for Scotland but no occasion was more memorable than in 1936 at Wembley, when Scotland trailed 1-0 to England and were awarded a penalty. In nerve-wracking circumstances, the 19 year-old Walker saw the ball blow off the penalty spot three times in the swirling wind before he calmly sent the kick into the net to give Scotland the draw needed to win the Home Championship. To those who knew him, it was no surprise that he trained for the ministry and he took that gentle

Tommy Walker with team-mates in the 1930s.

quality into management. Walker had a spell at Chelsea, where he was also a huge success, before he returned to Hearts to act as assistant manager and then manager.

Walker was, of course, lucky enough to have Alfie Conn, Willie Bauld and Jimmy Wardhaugh up front to score the goals that helped Hearts to their most potent period. The impact of 'The Terrible Trio' is documented elsewhere in this book but it would be wrong to assume Hearts were a three-man forward-line. Jimmy Murray also made his mark on the 1958 league title-winning team when he hit 27 goals in 33 matches. He also scored 11 when Hearts won the title again two years later and he played in the 1958 World Cup finals for Scotland in Sweden. To further endear him to Hearts supporters, he also netted twice in the 5-1 win over Partick Thistle in the 1958 League Cup Final. Gordon Smith, more noted as one of Hibs' *'Famous Five',* also spent time at Hearts and won a league medal in 1960, showing he still had plenty to offer.

Alex Young was one of the most naturally gifted players to put on a maroon shirt. Not only could he pass with precision but his close-control could pull any defence apart. But Young also had a talent for scoring - 24 in the league title-winning team of 1958, when he scored the goal which won the league at St Mirren - and then 23 in the 1959-60 campaign. Young is one of the few players to have won league and cup medals both in Scotland and in England, after he moved south to join Everton, where he was also hero-worshipped, at the end of 1960. His son Jason was also on Hearts books for a while.

Willie Wallace was another popular striker with the Tynecastle faithful. He led the scoring charts every season from 1962-67, including 1963-64, when he hit 30 goals. But he was allowed to join Celtic halfway through the 1966-67 season and, while it was a good move on his part as he won a European Cup winners' medal at the end of the season, he was sorely missed at Tynecastle.

Donald Ford was to fill his boots and was Hearts' top scorer for the next eight seasons. Also a gifted cricketer (although he did not play for Scotland in a full international), Ford was a slightly-built but energetic and brave striker whose pace was a handful for opposing defences. He scored 188 goals in 435 matches for Hearts, which was a handsome return and he was capped three times by Scotland. Unfortunately, there were no winners' medals for Ford to remember his Tynecastle career but he played in the 1968 Scottish Cup Final and the 1971 Texaco Cup Final and was one of the most feared strikers of his generation.

Drew Busby was another striker who gave his all for the club and was the perfect foil for Ford. He also formed a decent partnership with Willie Gibson and the duo shared 30 goals equally in 1975-76. Gibson was also a handful for defenders and, on one memorable occasion against Arbroath late in 1977, both Busby and Gibson scored a 'hat-trick' in a 7-0 win in the First Division. The goals were to help Hearts back into the Premier Division.

Once in the Premier Division, Hearts had the likes of Jimmy Bone, Sandy Clark, John Colquhoun and Scott Crabbe in their firing line and all four made a mark. Bone, in the twilight of his career, helped nurture John Robertson. Clark can also take credit for assisting Robertson and the two had a prolific pairing in 1985-86, when Hearts went within a whisker of the title. Colquhoun also had a terrific year that season and had Crabbe not been allowed to leave Tynecastle prematurely and then been hit by injuries, there is little doubt he would have pushed even Robertson in the scoring stakes.

In the eighties, however, it was Robertson who carved out a niche for himself as a goalscorer of immense consistency. Famously allowed to slip through the hands of Hibs after he had gained a reputation throughout Edinburgh schools' football of scoring goals for fun, he could score goals at any level and from any distance. Unfairly branded as a penalty box player by some people, he linked up well with the midfield and brought other players into the play. For a player who dominated the Hearts' goalscoring lists for the best part of 18 years, he had a high scoring

John Robertson celebrates another goal.

percentage for chances created and was an exceptionally intelligent football player. 'Robbo' had the knack of scoring regularly against the *'Old Firm'* and also seemed to take great delight in finding the net against Hibs. He won 16 caps for Scotland and never let the international side down when he played. While he does not like being compared with Willie Bauld, he surely stands comparison with the *'King of Hearts'* for the number of goals he scored at a time when football had become more defensive. Robertson is Hearts' record league scorer and his 214 goals will surely not be surpassed. In all, he made 632 appearances for the club and scored 271 goals. He had a brief spell at Newcastle which did not work out but was welcomed back to Tynecastle with open arms. Finally managing a winner's medal in the 1998 Scotish Cup Final, where he was a substitute, he joined Livingston that summer as player-coach.

Even without Robertson, there are plenty of goals left in Hearts. Neil McCann is a tricky winger with pace and control, who has been a stand-out since coming to Hearts and another former Dundee player, Jim Hamilton, has shown he knows the way to goal and will provide many great goals to come. French striker, Stephane Adam, whose 1998 Cup Final goal proved to be the winner, has adapted well to the Scottish game. He is also a workaholic on the park and is one of the shrewdest signings Jim Jefferies has made.

THE TERRIBLE TRIO

SELDOM can £200 have been invested more wisely in any Scottish football club. Dave McLean, who preceded Tommy Walker as manager of Hearts, had the distinction of signing all three of what became known as *'The Terrible Trio'* - Alfie Conn, Willie Bauld and Jimmy Wardhaugh - without having to dig too deeply into the Tynecastle coffers.

A more apt label may have been *'The Terrific Trio'*, as, signed within two years of each other, they went on to contribute 950 goals for Hearts, which brought the silverware that their supporters had craved for almost half a century. But 'terrible' they were for any defence to confront.

It is true that the team that matured under the managership of Walker was not without its other guiding influences, such as Dave Mackay, Freddie Glidden, John Cumming and Alex Young; but it was the astonishing goal deluge of Conn, Bauld and Wardhaugh that swamped defences throughout the country. Given that Conn stood just 5'7" and Bauld and Wardhaugh were both 5'8", what they achieved is even more remarkable.

Willie Bauld drinks from the Scottish Cup, 1956.

These three players were simply the right men at the right time for Hearts but it can also be argued that they were *ahead* of their time. Bauld, who had signed provisional forms with Sunderland as a youngster, spent all 16 years of his career at Hearts, Conn was at Tynecastle for 14 years and Wardhaugh for 13. For all their goals, the trio never represented Scotland together and it is remarkable that they only gathered six full caps between them, though Bauld would surely have amassed much more than his three, had it not been for injuries.

Conn was the first of the three to put pen to paper at Tynecastle. Born in Prestonpans, he signed as a 17 year-old in 1944. Jimmy Wardhaugh, born at Marshall Meadow, near Berwick, was next to arrive two years later but, within a month, Bauld, born in Newcraighall, had also signed after a mix-up over forms meant a proposed move to Sunderland fell through.

Bauld - still the undisputed *'King of Hearts'* - had to wait two-and-a-half years to make his first-team debut, as he was farmed out to Newtongrange Star and Edinburgh City to gain experience before he could pull on a maroon jersey for the senior team, just three months short of his 21st birthday. Bauld admitted that he was concerned he was about to be given a free transfer by Hearts when he was at Edinburgh City, then in the 'C' Division. But he conceded that he truly learned the game during his spell there.

In his testimonial booklet at the end of his career, Bauld revealed that he was depressed at the thought of joining Edinburgh City but then added that he did not regret it. *"It taught me that to run, you must first walk,"* he recalled. Bauld confessed that he did not know the secret of the success of the three-pronged partnership but that something just clicked.

"Alfie, Jimmy and I are often asked what the secret of our success as an inside trio was," he wrote in *'My Story'* in 1958, *"None of us knows. I doubt if the late Davie McLean knew either, although he was an astute judge of the game. It was said at the time that the introduction of our trio was one of the best things he did in his career. But I think these things just happen. There is that happy 'click' and things start coming off."*

It started coming off for Conn, Bauld and Wardhaugh from the moment they first set foot on a football pitch together. It was against East Fife, managed at the time by Scot Symon, who later was to take charge of Rangers, on October 9, 1948 at Tynecastle.

Hearts had taken just two points from their first six league matches and had recently lost 4-0 to East Fife at Bayview. Manager McLean had been chopping and changing his team and Conn and Wardhaugh had both been in and out of the team. McLean raised more than a few eyebrows by naming Conn at inside-right, Wardhaugh at inside-left and handing a debut to the little-known Bauld at centre-forward.

After 14 minutes of the League Cup tie, the *arms* were also raised, as Bauld marked his debut with a goal. A second followed in the 64th minute and, in the 74th minute, his 'hat-trick' was completed. Conn also scored two that day as Hearts won 6-1 (Dave Laing scored the other goal with a penalty).

As if that was not enough, Bauld scored a 'hat-trick' the following week in his second match for the first-team, against Queen of the South.

Conn was also on the scoresheet that afternoon in a 4-0 League Cup win. Wardhaugh and Conn supplied the goals the following week in a 2-0 league win over Rangers at Tynecastle in front of a 41,000 crowd. Bauld finished the season as top scorer with 24 goals, Conn contributed 16 and Wardhaugh 14 - a total of 54 goals in a season where Hearts scored 92 in all competitions. It was only a start.

Hearts finished eighth in the First Division that season (1948-49) but with Bauld scoring 40 goals the following season, Hearts climbed to a third-place finish behind Rangers and Hibernian, winning five of their last seven matches. The campaign included a 9-0 win over Falkirk at Tynecastle and ended with a 6-2 home win over Dundee (scorers: Bauld 3, Wardhaugh 2, Conn).

Wardhaugh went on to score a record 376 goals for the club in 518 matches, which is unlikely to be surpassed, Bauld notched 355 and Conn 221. Even at a time when goals flowed more easily in the Scottish League, it is a remarkable total. While John Robertson's modern-day tally of 271 in 632 appearances may fall some way short, it stands up to close scrutiny and Robertson is out on his own on league goals (214), after eclipsing Wardhaugh's 206 in the final game of the 1996-97 season, against Rangers.

Freddie Glidden cannot put his finger on why this Hearts vintage was so good but he recalls that there was a strong bond between the players. *"Most of us had come through the third team and the second team together and there was a great spirit in that team. We also had good trainers in John Harvey and Donald Macleod, who worked us really hard pre-season. Harvey had come from the army and it was his idea to use Gullane for training and not Jock Wallace, which is the popular belief. Jock was at Tynecastle as a coach and learned it from*

John and it was just that he had more publicity for doing it when he was at Rangers.

"In the fifties, we were lucky to get paid £10 a week, which does not compare with what players receive nowadays. There was no great gulf between our wages and those of the working man and we had to make our own way to 'home' games. Crowds of 35,000-40,000 were commonplace and football was just a way of life. Many of the supporters worked in the pits on the Saturday morning and then came straight to Tynecastle in the afternoon.

"There was not the same pressure on you to win as there is now. You just went out and played your best and we were not locked in the dressing-room for an hour if we lost or anything like that."

For a club that had not won a major piece of silverware since 1906, there was a feeling that the patience of the supporters would at last be rewarded in the not-too-distant future. Tragically, manager McLean was not able to see his team reach their potential as he died in February, 1951. His mantle was taken over by his assistant Tommy Walker, who had returned to Tynecastle after two years at Chelsea and went on to guide Hearts through the most successful spell in their history.

THE RECORDS

JIMMY WARDHAUGH 1946-59

	Games	Goals
League:	304	206
League Cup:	78	43
Scottish Cup:	36	21
Others:	98 + 2(sub)	106
Total:	**516 + 2(sub)**	**376**

WILLIE BAULD 1948-62

	Games	Goals
League:	292	183
League Cup:	76	70
Scottish Cup:	40	22
Others:	102 + 1(sub)	80
Total:	**510 + 1(sub)**	**355**

ALFIE CONN 1944-58

	Games	Goals
League:	240	122
League Cup:	65	28
Scottish Cup:	33	15
Others:	69 + 1(sub)	56
Total:	**407 + 1(sub)**	**221**

(These figures have been verified by Hearts' historians and amended since 1984).

THE GROWTH OF HEARTS

TOMMY WALKER spent 15 years as manager of the club he once graced so well as a player and during that time, Hearts returned to the winners' rostrum. The 'silver streak' yielded seven trophies in nine years, including two League Championships in 1958 and 1960. Outside of the *'Old Firm'*, only Aberdeen in the 1980s have bettered that trophy haul.

In an illustrious playing career with Hearts and Chelsea, Walker had won everything in the way of plaudits but nothing in the way of medals. Yet, as a manager, he clearly had the alchemist's touch and the long wait for a trophy finally came to an end in 1954 when Hearts beat Motherwell 4-2 in the League Cup Final at Hampden.

Hearts scored a total of 34 goals on the way to the trophy, with Willie Bauld helping himself to a dozen. Hearts beat Celtic 'home' and 'away' in their qualifying section and even a 4-1 loss to Dundee at Dens Park could not prevent them reaching the quarter finals. St Johnstone were removed 7-0 on aggregate and Hearts secured their final place with a 4-1 win over Airdrie at Easter Road, with Jimmy Wardhaugh scoring twice and Bauld also on the scoresheet.

And so it was on to Hampden on October 23 and it was more than curiosity as to whether Hearts could end 48 years of separation from a trophy that drew a crowd of 55,640.

Motherwell had beaten Rangers on the way to the final and had won the Scottish Cup two years earlier but Hearts, and Bauld in particular, it seemed, were anxious to finally give their supporters something to savour. He netted twice in the first quarter-of-an-hour to put Hearts in control and, even after Willie Redpath pulled one back from the penalty spot after Wilson Humphries had been fouled, Wardhaugh made it 3-1 before half-time with a header.

Bauld completed his 'hat-trick' in the 88th minute and a consolation goal for Motherwell from Alex Bain was not to drown the maroon cheers. When Bobby Parker collected the cup after the final whistle, it finally ended the years of jokes in Edinburgh about Hearts' aversion to anything silver.

What a welcome Hearts received when they returned to Edinburgh with the cup, as Gorgie celebrated long into the night. As Albert Mackie recalled in his 1959 book, *'The Hearts'*:

"Every window was crammed. The old grey-stone walls, the smoke-blackened walls, reverberated with the wave after wave of cheering. Women threw maroon rosettes to the team as if to Spanish toreadors. At McLeod Street, where part of the Saturday crowd surges into Tynecastle, there were crowds of people singing outside the public-house where the fans have their last hurried pint on their way to the match and their first to celebrate victory or drown their sorrows afterwards. This time it was undoubted and crowning victory, and the foaming tumblers of good strong Edinburgh ale slopped over as they were raised in salute."

This was more than a Cup Final win; this was a moment in history for Heart of Midlothian Football Club. If there had been any doubt that Tommy Walker would achieve legendary status after a playing career that brought 20 Scotland caps, then it was removed by this victory. Even if the League Cup was a relatively new tournament (it was only instigated after World War II), such a triumph bridged the 48-year gap with the Hearts team that won the Scottish Cup in 1906.

The Scottish Cup had not been to an Edinburgh engraver since that 1906 win (Hibs last won it in 1902) and Hearts had since been to the final only once - in 1907 when they were roundly beaten 3-0 by Celtic - but, less than two years after hoisting the League Cup, the Scottish Cup was paraded down Gorgie way.

This time, both halves of the *'Old Firm'* had to be negotiated - Rangers in the quarter finals and Celtic in the final. The cup campaign started with a 3-0 win over Forfar Athletic at

Tynecastle, with Alfie Conn (2) and Johnny Hamilton getting the goals. Next was Stirling Albion at Tynecastle and this time Hearts thrashed in five goals without reply - Bauld, Cumming, Young, Conn and Wardhaugh–to set up a 'home' quarter final with Rangers.

Hearts won convincingly 4-0, with two goals in each half, Bauld (2), Crawford and Conn all getting on the scoresheet. The semi-final tie with Raith Rovers was played at Easter Road and

Hearts squad, 1958.

it took a replay - after a 0-0 draw - to book the final place, as Hearts, even without the injured Conn, romped through 3-0, with Wardhaugh (2) and Crawford on the mark. Five matches, fifteen goals and a defence that had not been breached put Hearts in confident mood for the final with Celtic on April 21, 1956.

A massive 133,339 crowd jammed Hampden that afternoon, around 50,000 making their way from Edinburgh. There were not enough tickets to meet demand and a few thousand were locked out. With Bobby Parker injured, Freddie Glidden captained Hearts and, within 20 minutes of winning the toss, he watched as Ian Crawford slotted in the opening goal. At the end of the first half, John Cumming suffered a badly cut eye after a clash with Willie Fernie but battled on bravely to help steer Hearts to victory. Crawford scored again and, though Michael Haughney pulled one back for Celtic, Bauld set up Conn to fire in the decisive goal with ten minutes left.

That evening, the Ministry of Works authorised the floodlighting of Edinburgh Castle to celebrate the 3-1 victory at Hampden and hostelries in the Royal Mile, where large crowds had gathered, were giving free drinks to regulars. The coach that took the triumphant team back from Glasgow stopped off along the way at Blackburn, in West Lothian, where Freddie Glidden's mother and father toasted the win, at Livingston Station, where Tommy Walker was born, and then to Newbridge, where Bobby Parker, who missed the final due to a cartilage operation, was raised.

The league title was next - in 1958. The previous season, Hearts had been pipped by Rangers for the title. Rangers were two points behind with two games in hand and, although Hearts won their final two matches, Rangers took full points from their last four to take the title by just two points. There was to be no mistake the following season.

Hearts only lost one league match (a 2-1 defeat by Clyde at Shawfield in November) and won the title with 13 points to spare over second-placed Rangers. During a season when Hearts were at their most potent, there was only one occasion when they failed to score in the league (a 0-0 draw with Third Lanark in October) but big winning margins were commonplace - 7-2 v Airdrie, 9-0 v East Fife, 8-0 v Queen's Park, 9-1 v Falkirk and 7-2 v Third Lanark.

Hearts scored a record 132 league goals - beating the previous record of 119 set by Motherwell in 1932 - and conceded just 29. An ankle injury meant Alfie Conn played in just five matches and, in a season where Hearts scored so freely, it is interesting to note that Willie Bauld played in only nine matches. Alex Young was preferred to Bauld at centre-forward for many weeks and Jimmy Murray also slotted in to a new-look 'terrible trio' of Murray, Young and Wardhaugh.

The three amassed 79 of the 132 goals between them, while Conn - who had the distinction of scoring Hearts' 100th league goal of the season against Motherwell - and Bauld managed just nine between them. In one spell, Murray scored 27 goals in 33 matches and the team, superbly led by new young captain, Dave Mackay, were in a class of their own.

Bauld admitted that it had been a major disappointment to him that he had not played a greater part in Hearts' first league title for 61 years. *"It will always remain a great regret that I did not play a bigger part in Hearts' fabulous and long overdue league triumph,"* he was to say afterwards. *"The achievement, as our chairman, Mr Nicol Kilgour, has often pointed out, was due essentially to team-work."*

Hearts won the title again two years later, when Bauld played in 17 games and scored 10 goals but, by then, Conn had departed and signed for Raith Rovers for £3,000 and the dismantling of the *'Terrible Trio'* had started. Wardhaugh was then permitted to leave after 13 years and 375 goals, when Dunfermline were successful with a £2,000 bid after it had been rumoured that Hibs were interested in taking him across the city.

Wardhaugh and Bauld both played in the team that won the League Cup in 1958 with a 5-1 final win over Partick Thistle - Bauld scoring twice and Murray (2) and Johnny Hamilton scoring the others - but Hearts were unable to retain their title. Dave Mackay departed to Tottenham Hotspur for £32,000 in the March, at a time when Hearts were sitting six points behind Rangers. Many felt that Mackay's departure had handed Rangers the league but, going into the final Saturday, Hearts could still win the title if Rangers lost to Aberdeen and they managed to beat Celtic. As it turned out, Aberdeen kept their half of the bargain with a 2-1 victory but Hearts lost by the same score to Celtic and, not for the last time, the league flag was to prove elusive on the final day of a season.

But Hearts had proved they could be winners and the Tynecastle fans had grown accustomed to victory parades. Another League Cup was won in 1959, this time with a 2-1 final win over Third Lanark. A mistake by goalkeeper, Gordon Marshall, had enabled Matt Gray to give Third Lanark an early lead but Hamilton equalised with the help of a deflection early in the second half and Young scored the winning goal shortly afterwards. Earning a winner's medal that afternoon was Gordon Smith, who had been allowed to leave Hibs, prematurely as it turned out. A crowd of 12,000 had turned out to watch him in his first reserve fixture for Hearts and he went on to play in 29 league matches as Hearts recaptured the title.

The only disappointment of the season was a first-round exit in the Scottish Cup to Kilmarnock after a replay but Hearts pipped the Ayrshire side for the league title, losing only three of their 34 matches and again scoring more than a hundred goals (102).

Hearts finished only eighth in the 1960-61 season, 17 points behind champions, Rangers, and also struggled to make an impact in the cup competitions, not making it through the qualifying stages of the League Cup and going out of the Scottish Cup at the quarter-final stage to St Mirren. After losing in the 1961 League Cup Final replay to Rangers - a John Cumming penalty gave Hearts a 1-1 draw in the first game (when a 17 year-old Alan Gordon was surprisingly preferred to Bauld in attack) but a Norrie Davidson goal was all Hearts had to show for a 3-1 replay defeat inspired by Jim Baxter - Hearts' last silverware under Tommy Walker (and what was to be their last trophy for 36 years) came on October 27, 1962.

By that stage, Walker had rebuilt his team. Conn, Bauld and Wardhaugh had all departed, as had Alex Young, who had joined Everton along with George Thomson in a joint £58,000 deal. Bauld had been given a free transfer after 16 years at Tynecastle at the end of the 1961-62 season and had decided to retire from the game, the last of his 356 goals coming against Third Lanark in a 2-1 win in the February.

As Brian Scott recounts in his book, '*The Terrible Trio*', Bauld's testimonial match with Sheffield United, which drew a crowd of 15,000 in November 1962, was a bitter-sweet parting. The player was presented with a cheque for £2,800 but expenses were deducted, which left him with just £1,700. It was fully 12 years before he returned to the ground.

So it was a rebuilt Hearts team that faced Kilmarnock in the League Cup Final of that year. Willie Wallace, who within five years was to win a European Cup medal with Celtic, was the new goal king and he hit a 'hat-trick' in the 4-0 demolition of St Johnstone in the semi final at Easter Road. But it was Norrie Davidson who supplied the only goal of the final when he accepted a cutback from Willie Hamilton to score in the 26th minute. But the game will also be remembered for a controversial refereeing decision by Tom Wharton, who disallowed what had seemed like a decent equaliser from Frank Beattie in the final minute. It was a lucky break but luck was to be something that was in short supply for Hearts for many years to come.

THOSE EUROPEAN NIGHTS

NOT SINCE 1983 has a Scottish club lifted a European trophy and the possibility of another team emulating what Celtic, Rangers and Aberdeen have achieved in the past has looked increasingly remote. For all the millions of pounds that Rangers and Celtic have invested in European-reared players in recent years, success on the European stage seems harder to come by than ever.

Hearts cannot lay claim to coming close to joining that trio but there has not been a shortage of European memories to cherish under the Tynecastle floodlights and even on foreign fields. The 'luck' of the draw has seen such giants as Standard Liege, Benfica, Inter Milan, Paris St Germain, Bayern Munich, Atletico Madrid and Red Star Belgrade visit Gorgie.

Apart from Benfica and Inter Milan, only Hamburg and FC Liege had won at Tynecastle at the time of going to print which is a measure of how Hearts have managed to raise their game when confronted by such opposition through the years. There were memorable nights at Tynecastle when Hearts dramatically swept aside first-leg deficits to overwhelm Lokomotiv Leipzig and Slavia Prague.

But the most notable scalp must be the night when the mighty Bayern Munich were beaten at Tynecastle in a UEFA Cup quarter-final tie in 1989. Under Alex MacDonald's expert guidance (MacDonald had been a key figure for Rangers when they won the European Cup-Winners' Cup in Barcelona in 1972), Hearts stunned the famous German side, which included Klaus Augenthaler, Stefan Reuter and Olaf Thon, with a goal fit to win any game. Iain Ferguson, a player with the capacity to produce the most splendid goals, steered in a 25-yard shot after a short free-kick from Tosh McKinlay. Hearts were desperately unlucky in the second leg in Munich, when John Colquhoun hit a post as Hearts sought an 'away goal'. As it turned out, goals from Augenthaler, as sweet a strike as Ferguson's in the first leg, and Erland Johnsen, a header, saw Bayern through on a 2-1 aggregate.

It brought an end to a fine European run which had seen Hearts beat St Patrick's from Dublin (4-0 aggregate), Austria Vienna (1-0 aggregate) and Bosnia's Velez Mostar (4-2 aggregate). Hearts looked as if they had lost their chance in the second round when they drew 0-0 at Tynecastle with the Austrians but they produced a disciplined performance in the return at the Prater Stadium and were rewarded when Mike Galloway headed in the winning goal after Walter Kidd had accepted a long pass from Eamonn Bannon. The goal had more than a hint of offside about it when both Kidd and Galloway galloped clear of the Austrian defence together but the goal was to stand. It was also a night for defender Jimmy Sandison to prove his ability as a marker, as he stifled the threat of the celebrated Austrian midfield player Herbert Prohaska.

Manager MacDonald had given Sandison a photograph of the player in the build-up to the match and Jimmy never let him out of his sights all night. He even had the photograph in his top pocket when he spoke with journalists at the airport before the team returned home, such was his dedication to duty. An interested observer in the stands that evening was Thomas Flogel, then a young player with Vienna who was later to sign for Hearts.

Mike Galloway, later to sign for Celtic before a car accident cruelly cut short his career, scored five goals on that European run, including an invaluable one in Mostar when Hearts escaped with a 1-2 defeat on one of the most intimidating European nights, to go through 4-2 on aggregate after first-leg goals from Eamonn Bannon, Galloway and John Colquhoun.

John Robertson was a notable absentee for most of the European run - his only involvement was as a substitute in Munich's Olympic Stadium - as he had joined Newcastle but, helped by the money accrued by the successful run, Hearts brought him back for £750,000, with the deal concluded on the night of the match in Mostar.

Hearts' first flirtation with European football was not a happy one as they were destroyed 5-1 by Standard Liege in Belgium in the 1958-59 European Cup, with Ian Crawford claiming the club's first European goal and a 2-1 victory in the return - courtesy of a brace from Willie Bauld - was never going to be enough. Hearts were again involved in Europe's premier competition in 1960-61 but drew Portuguese champions, Benfica, who went on to win the trophy that season. Benfica led 2-0 in front of 29,500 fans in the first leg at Tynecastle before Alex Young pulled one back late on but the second leg in Lisbon proved too great an obstacle and Hearts went down 3-0 to go out on a 5-1 aggregate.

Hearts finally won through a round in Europe the following season when they defeated Luxembourg's Union St Gilloise in the first round of the old Inter-Cities Fairs Cup (now the UEFA Cup) on a 5-1 aggregate, winning 3-1 'away' and 2-0 at 'home'. It set up a second-round meeting with Inter Milan and the Italians frustrated Hearts with their defensive tactics to take a 1-0 win from the first leg in Edinburgh and follow it up with a 4-0 win in Italy, which, along with an identical defeat by Paris St Germain in the same competition in 1984, is Hearts' worst European defeat.

Hearts' only other sojourns into Europe in the sixties ended in play-off defeats by Swiss side, Lausanne, in 1963-64 and Spanish cracks, Real Zarragoza, in 1965-66 and there was no progress beyond the third round. In 1965, Hearts had been given a first round 'bye' and then put out the Norwegian side Valerengens 4-1 on aggregate to set up the tie with Zarragoza. The Spaniards had won the Fairs Cup in 1964 and brought a formidable line-up to Tynecastle but Hearts, 0-2 down at half-time, stormed back to lead 3-2 with goals from Alan Anderson, Don Kerrigan and Willie Wallace before Zarragoza tied it up at 3-3. A 2-2 draw in Spain - Anderson and Wallace were again on the mark - where Danny Ferguson was injured, leaving Hearts with ten men (there were no substitutes in those days), meant a play-off and, with Hearts losing the toss of the coin, a return to Spain, where the Scots went out 1-0.

It was season 1976-77 before Hearts had to look out their passports again and it looked like the earliest of exits when Hearts lost 2-0 away to German side, Lokomotiv Leipzig, in the first round of the Cup-winners' Cup. But Hearts produced a stirring response in the second leg - Roy Kay pulled one back after just a dozen minutes and Willie Gibson added a second shortly afterwards to level the tie. Leipzig scored a valuable 'away goal' before half-time and it looked like another familiar hard-luck tale. But Hearts stuck to the task and second-half goals from Jim Brown, Drew Busby and Gibson again gave Tynecastle a rare night to savour.

When Hearts lost 4-2 in the first leg of their second-round match to SV Hamburg in Germany, there were high hopes of a repeat of the first round, especially as Hearts had scored two 'away goals' through Busby and Donald Park. A 25,000 crowd packed Tynecastle for the return but Hamburg produced a clinical display and killed off the tie by scoring twice before half-time, which meant Hearts had to find five in the second half to win. A goal from Gibson could not turn the tide and the Germans ran out 4-1 winners on the night.

It was another eight years before Hearts were involved in Europe again and this time a 4-0 first-leg defeat by Paris St Germain at the Parc des Princes meant a double from John Robertson in the second leg was academic, as the French side went through to the second round of the UEFA Cup on a 6-2 aggregate. Hearts were rather more unfortunate in 1986-87 when they lost out on 'away goals' to Dukla Prague - winning 3-2 at home (Sandy Clark, Wayne Foster and Robertson) but losing 1-0 away.

After the fantastic run in 1988-89, Hearts were on UEFA Cup business again in 1990-91, when Sandy Clark was caretaker-manager following the sacking of Alex MacDonald. He took the team to the little-known Ukrainian outpost of Dnepropetrovsk to face Dnepr and came away with a creditable 1-1 draw, with Robertson again netting. Chairman, Wallace Mercer, had missed the trip to secure MacDonald's replacement and it was while Hearts were away that news leaked out that Joe Jordan had been appointed manager. Hearts, with Jordan at the helm, comfortably won the second leg 3-1, with goals from Robertson (2) and Dave McPherson and there was also a fine 3-1 home win over Italian side Bologna in the next round (Foster 2 and Iain Ferguson). Jordan, who had made such an impact in his playing days with AC Milan, was much sought after by Italian reporters when Hearts arrived in Bologna for the second leg but there was to be no famous victory and the Italians scored two late goals to win the game 3-0 and book their place in the third round.

Hearts returned to Prague in season 1992-93 to face Slavia Prague in the UEFA Cup and came away with a narrow 1-0 defeat. The return had it all - six goals and a sending-off for Slavia's Penicka. Hearts led 3-1 on the night with goals from Gary Mackay, Ian Baird and Craig Levein but Slavia scored another crucial 'away goal', which meant Hearts required another. It was the unlikely boot of midfield player Glyn Snodin that supplied it with a thunderous 30-yard free-kick, which remains one of the finest European goals seen at Tynecastle. Hearts progressed to face FC Liege, guided by Dutch legend, Arie Haan, who made some uncomplimentary remarks about Hearts before the tie. The Belgians won both legs 1-0 but not before Hearts had given Haan's side a scare or two, particularly in the return in Liege.

Sandy Clark succeeded Jordan as manager and, after doing so well as caretaker against Dnepr, he was given a juicy first European tie as full-time manager when Hearts were drawn against Atletico Madrid in the 1993-94 UEFA Cup. Late goals from Robertson and Colquhoun put Hearts 2-0 up in the first leg at Tynecastle but the home side left the door ajar at the back and Polish international, Roman Kesecki, scored a precious goal for the Spanish side before the finish. The second leg was always going to be difficult and a strong second-half display took Atletico through 3-0 and 4-2 on aggregate.

Jim Jefferies was also handed big-name opposition in his first taste of Europe, when Hearts drew Red Star Belgrade in the preliminary round of the Cup-Winners' Cup in 1996-97. The manager enjoyed testing himself tactically against such a revered name and Hearts gained a laudable 0-0 draw in Belgrade before they had even started their domestic campaign. A Dave McPherson header gave Hearts the advantage in the second leg but a second-half goal from Dino

Marinovic in a bruising encounter was enough to put Red Star through on the 'away goals' rule.

But such an outcome did not diminish Hearts' appetite for European fare and the anticipation is as keen as ever for some more of those special Tynecastle nights.

That was evident when Hearts recorded what is their biggest European win to date when they overwhelmed Estonian side, FC Lantana, 5-0 at Tynecastle in the preliminary round of the 1998-99 Cup Winners' Cup. A crowd of over 15,000 turned up to witness the encounter and were rewarded with goals from Jim Hamilton, Neil McCann, Steve Fulton, Thomas Flogel and Derek Holmes, which put Hearts through on a 6-0 aggregate.

Picture Gallery

Players return with the League Cup, 1958.

Duff, McKenzie, Bauld, Wardhaugh, Glidden & Crawford with Scottish Cup won by Hearts, 1956.

Conn, Cumming & Young with the Scottish Cup, 1956.

Fans invade Hampden after winning the cup.

Murray & Battles.

The Duke of Gloucester visits Tynecastle, 1958.

Walter Kidd & Dave McPherson.

Craig Levein.

Alan Mclaren

Neil Berry

Gary Locke

Giles Rousset

Cameron scores from the penalty spot.

Steve Fulton with the Scottish Cup.

Jim Jefferies with the Scottish Cup.

Scenes back in Gorgie Road.

Paul Ritchie and Gordon Durie clash.

Celebrations back at Tynecastle.

Management and bench celebrate.

Players and fans celebrate.

Jubilant Ritchie.

Jim Hamilton and Stephane Adam with the Scottish Cup, 1998.

Neil McCann and David Weir .

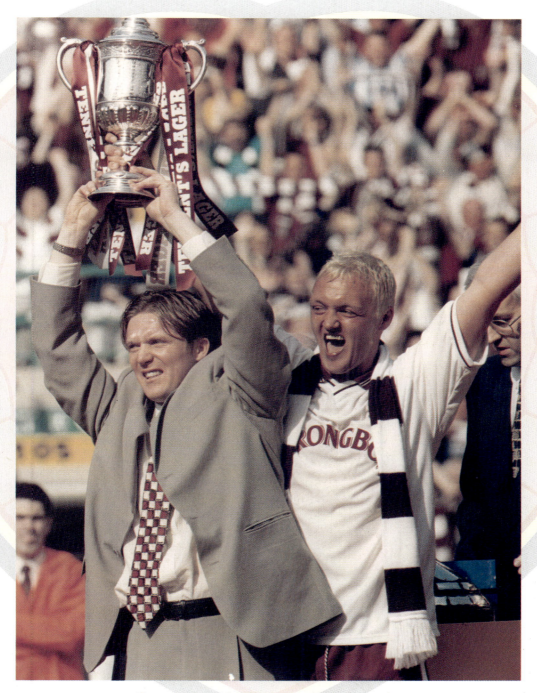

Gary Locke and Steve Fulton with the trophy.

Colin Cameron and Neil McCann.

Flogel and Ritchie continue to celebrate.

Hearts Squad, 1968.

Hearts Squad, 1971/72.

Deadly duo of Robertson and Colquhoun.

Neil McCann.

CAPITAL LOSSES, CAPITAL GAINS

THE GODS clearly felt Hearts needed to serve some penance for the luck they rode in the 1962 League Cup Final but few could have predicted how severe that would be. It should have been more than sufficient for Hearts to surrender the league title on the last day of the 1964-65 season in the most traumatic fashion - to Kilmarnock, no less - but the suffering was to last 36 years.

It was to involve several final hurdle falls. In 1965, it was 'goal average' that cost Hearts the league and, ironically, after they had successfully implored the Scottish League to change the system, the title was lost on 'goal difference' in 1986. There were also three Scottish Cup Final defeats to endure before the 1998 success and numerous semi-final defeats where Hearts managed to lose by every conceivable means, from goalkeeping errors to 'penalty shoot-outs.' There was also a League Cup Final defeat by Rangers which swung on a controversial refereeing decision. How the fates conspired to put Hearts supporters through the emotional blender. The chairmen changed, the managers changed and the players changed but the luck remained the same until Jim Jefferies turned it in 1998.

What went wrong in 1965 is difficult to dissect. A 7-1 home defeat by Dundee at the end of February put a question mark over whether Hearts could go the distance in the Championship but the team responded and, going into the final game against Kilmarnock, had only dropped one point - against Dundee United - in seven matches. So it was that over 37,000 fans turned up at Tynecastle on April 24, knowing a draw or even a one-goal defeat would be enough for Hearts to take the title. Hearts hit the post early on through Raold Jensen but their character was put to the test when Dave Sneddon headed Kilmarnock in front in the 27th minute. Worse was to follow. Within two minutes, Brian McIlroy shot Kilmarnock further ahead. Hearts had their chances in the second half but none was taken and Kilmarnock were crowned champions by virtue of a better 'goal average' than Hearts - just 0.04. The recovery from that setback was slow.

Tommy Walker resigned in 1966 and was succeeded by trainer, John Harvey. He took Hearts to the 1968 Scottish Cup Final against Dunfermline with a campaign which included a quarter-final win over Rangers. The lowest Cup Final crowd since the war (56,365) saw Dunfermline win 3-1, through goals from Pat Gardner (2) and Ian Lister (penalty) and Hearts' only counter came from an own-goal by John Lunn.

Hearts finished 12th in the league that year and indeed only managed a top-five finish once - in 1970, when they were fourth - before the old First Division gave way to the Premier League in 1975-76. With European football outwith their grasp, Hearts took part in a new competition, an Anglo-Scottish Cup, which was initially sponsored by Texaco and open to teams from both sides of the border who had missed out on Europe.

In the inaugural year of 1970-71, Hearts reached the final after a tense two-leg semi final with Motherwell. A crowd of over 25,000 turned up for the first leg of the final against Wolves at Tynecastle. Hearts lost 3-1, with Donald Ford scoring and, although they performed well in the return at Molineux and won 1-0 thanks to a goal from George Fleming, the damage had been done in the first leg. Hearts took part in the competition for the next five years but failed to progress beyond the second round on any occasion.

The early seventies proved difficult for Hearts and, on New Year's Day in 1973, there was an embarrassing 7-0 home defeat by arch-rivals, Hibernian, which was to haunt the club for years to come. In the first season of the Premier Division, 1975-76, a fifth-place finish and a Scottish Cup Final against Rangers suggested that better times were ahead but closer scrutiny provided a more sobering picture. Hearts, in fact, had won only 13 of their 36 league games and were just three points better off than relegated Dundee at the end of the season.

The Scottish Cup Final was less than a minute old when Derek Johnstone headed in a free-kick from Tommy McLean after a foul by Jim Jefferies. Alex MacDonald volleyed in a second goal before half-time and Johnstone added his second and Rangers' third in the 63rd minute. All Hearts managed was a consolation goal from Graham Shaw moments later but it was too little, too late. The following year, Hearts were relegated for the first time in their 103-year history and their fate was virtually sealed when they lost 3-1 at home to a Rangers team that included MacDonald and Sandy Jardine, later to become managers of the club. Jardine, indeed, slotted in a penalty kick that afternoon and two draws with Hibs and Kilmarnock confirmed that Hearts were relegated. These were dark days indeed and, just a month beforehand, legendary centre-forward Willie Bauld had died suddenly at the age of 49, having taken ill through the night after attending a function at the Longstone Hearts Supporters' Club.

John Hagart, who had succeeded Bobby Seith as manager, resigned and was replaced by Willie Ormond. The former Hibernian forward was not wholly accepted by the Hearts support and, with the club hitting hard times on and off the pitch, the club was at the crossroads. Promotion back to the Premier League was won in 1978 (perhaps predictably, the First Division title was lost on 'goal difference' to Morton) but Hearts went straight back down in 1979. In 1980, Hearts, now under the management of Bobby Moncur, won the First Division title but the following season, finished bottom of the Premier League. This 'yo-yoing' did nothing for the financial stability of the club and major change was imminent.

Hearts were at their lowest ebb and efforts to raise money by the then chairman, Archie Martin, had failed and a momentous decision was taken to release 350,000 shares and effectively put the club up for sale. There followed a battle for control between Kenny Waugh, an Edinburgh bookmaker, later to become chairman of Hibs, and Wallace Mercer, a property developer, whose cause was championed by former centre-forward, Donald Ford. The battle went all the way to the wire and was widely reported by the Scottish national newspapers but it was Mercer who was given the vote on a 3-2 boardroom decision after raising the necessary £350,000. Given Hearts' predicament, he later conceded the day he gained control was, *both a nightmare and a dream come true.*

The flamboyant Mercer heralded a 'new Hearts' and his ebullient nature immediately breathed new life into the ailing club. Mercer took over on June 3, 1981, at the age of 34 and quickly showed himself to be at ease with the media. Mercer was to stamp his personality on the club for the next 13 years and while *The Scotsman* observed on the day of his appointment that there was a touch of Phineas T. Barnum about the new owner, his entrance was what the club required when it was facing financial hardship. *"In order to prosper, we must create cash and that means using methods other than putting eleven players on the field once a fortnight for 'home' games,"* he said on the day he took over. *"The cash must be used in turn to create custom because, without spectators, the game has nothing to offer."* At a time when Scottish football was just waking up to commercial sponsorship, Mercer gave Hearts a higher profile with some unique money-raising schemes, one of which included raffling a new house.

He would be the first to admit that he made some mistakes in his 13 years at Tynecastle, most spectacularly when he proposed a merger with city rivals, Hibs, which led to threats on his life from some more extreme Hibs supporters. He maintained at the time that he won the business argument but lost the emotional one but the move touched a raw nerve and, in retrospect, hurt Mercer's credibility. The move also upset Hearts supporters and even John Robertson, the club's most popular player at the time, showed up at a 'Hands Off Hibs' rally.

However, Mercer had a profound influence on Hearts and was, latterly, subject to unfair criticism. His dynamism helped transform Hearts and he had the personality to take the club by the scruff of its neck, drag it back to the top table and give it back its ambition. Maybe he held onto the reins for too long in the end but he gave the big-time feeling back to a club which had been stagnating since the departure of Tommy Walker.

Whether Mercer knew the enormity of what he was taking on at the time is debatable and change was inevitable when he first took over. Bobby Moncur, who deserves credit for realising the importance of a youth policy and notably signed John Robertson, Gary Mackay and Dave Bowman, resigned and was replaced by Tony Ford after Mercer had approached both Jim McLean and Jock Wallace about the position. The club spent £300,000 bringing in new players to help them out of the First Division but Mercer admitted afterwards that it was money that they did not have. After a run of poor results, Ford was sacked and Alex MacDonald was given the role of player-manager. But again the season was to end in frustration. A Steve Hancock goal gave Forfar a shock 1-0 Scottish Cup win at Tynecastle on February 13, 1982, which brought more dark clouds, the only silver lining being that the aforementioned Robertson was hastened into his debut four days later, when he came on as a 17 year-old substitute in a 4-1 win over Queen of the South. But May was the cruellest month. A 5-2 defeat by Dumbarton, a 0-0 draw with Kilmarnock and a 1-0 defeat by Motherwell meant Hearts missed promotion by one point.

There was crowd trouble at Rugby Park in the goalless draw and also in the 'home' defeat by Motherwell and Mercer had to leave his seat in the directors' box during the latter to appeal for calm. The ugly scenes were to have a deep impact on Mercer and he later said: *"That strength of feeling has always stayed with me. It was the one thing I didn't have on the balance-sheet."* Mercer knew that if this depth of feeling could be channelled in the right direction, then it could help pull Hearts out of their situation.

MacDonald also learned the managerial ropes quickly and Hearts finally secured promotion back to the Premier Division in 1983 as runners-up to St Johnstone and this time there was to be more permanence about their residence in the top division. The shrewd MacDonald also proved something of a revelation in the transfer, or rather free-transfer, market. Sandy Jardine, Willie Johnston, Donald Park and Jimmy Bone were all recruited for no fee and when money was available, he used it wisely. Players such as Craig Levein, Mike Galloway, Wayne Foster, Brian Whittaker, Kenny Black, Sandy Clark, John Colquhoun and Neil Berry were all brought in at little expense and yet all were to prove great servants to the club. Hearts won their first five matches in the Premier Division - including a 3-2 win over Hibs - to take the top league by storm and the momentum was enough to carry them to a fifth-place finish and a UEFA Cup place.

Hearts finished seventh in the league the following season and were beaten in the semi finals of the League Cup by Dundee United but there was no hint of the drama that was to unfold in 1985-86. A 1-1 draw with Celtic on the opening day of the season, followed by defeats by St Mirren (2-6) and Rangers (1-3), was their worst start to a league campaign for seven years but things were soon to change. After successive defeats by Motherwell and Clydebank in September, Hearts embarked on a 31-match unbeaten run which included a third-round Scottish Cup win over Rangers and a run of eight successive wins through March and April, taking them to the Scottish Cup Final and the brink of their first Championship since 1960.

A late equaliser from John Colquhoun against Aberdeen in April and a single-goal win over Clydebank, courtesy of an explosive shot from Gary Mackay, appeared to put Hearts outwith Celtic's reach at the top of the league. Hearts just needed to avoid defeat against Dundee at Dens Park on May 3 to take the title and even a narrow defeat would be enough provided Davie Hay's Celtic did not beat St Mirren by a huge margin in *their* final match. Over 10,000 Hearts supporters made the journey to Dundee expecting a celebration but by 4.40pm, it had become a wake. Two goals from Albert Kidd in the final seven minutes gave Dundee a 2-0 win after Hearts were denied what had looked like a clear penalty earlier in the match and Celtic rose to the occasion at Love Street by thrashing in five goals without reply. A virus that disrupted preparations meant Craig Levein missed the match and had to endure the misery of listening to events unfolding on the radio at home. It was a heartbreaking end to a league season which had produced many memorable moments and the fact that Hearts had lost the title again on the final day - as in 1965 - made it more difficult to take.

Dens Park had never known such desolation from visiting fans and the tears flowed freely on the terraces as the supporters struggled to take in what had happened. Alex MacDonald had never taken a title win for granted, even when it looked inevitable and it was a feature of his post-match press conferences that he played down talk of being champions. It proved to be a wise tactic.

Seven days later, the Scottish Cup Final was lost 3-0 to Aberdeen, with captain Walter Kidd sent off, to complete one of the darkest weeks in the history of the club. In the aftermath, MacDonald was keen to stress the positive side and pointed out that the club could still feel a sense of achievement at finishing runners-up in two of the three major competitions in only their third season back in the top division.

Hearts were back at Hampden the following season for a Scottish Cup semi final with St Mirren but, in spite of a fabulous goal from Gary Mackay, they were disappointingly beaten 2-1 by the eventual winners. There was arguably a more painful defeat in the 1988 semi final against Celtic, when Hearts looked set for victory after a freak goal from Brian Whittaker in the second half. But, with just three minutes left, goalkeeper Henry Smith erred badly and Mark McGhee equalised. Worse was to follow as Celtic snatched victory when Smith again blundered and Andy Walker scored the winning goal. In the league, Hearts had finished runners-up again, albeit a rather distant ten points behind Celtic. It was built on a solid defence - with Dave McPherson slotting in admirably - and Hearts lost just one of their last eleven league games and only four goals in that period.

Under Alex MacDonald's guidance, Hearts had their best run in Europe the following season when they reached the quarter-finals of the UEFA Cup before going down narrowly to the mighty Bayern Munich in a season which also saw them reach the semi finals of the League Cup (where they lost 3-0 to Rangers). But league form was patchy under the weight of the European commitments, although Hearts were able to re-sign John Robertson after his sojourn in England with Newcastle United. Hearts struggled in front of goal all season in the league and eventually had to be content with a sixth-place finish.

Hearts finished third in the league the following season but were only pipped for runners-up spot by Rangers on 'goal difference' and, with gates averaging 15,700 and with a lively if diminutive, front trio of Robertson, Scott Crabbe and John Colquhoun, there was a feeling that Hearts were at last poised to make a strike on the league title that had eluded them so cruelly in 1986. The new 'terrible trio' were at their best in a 4-0 Scottish Cup destruction of Motherwell in February and shared the goals between them.

But the following season started disappointingly with a 3-0 League Cup exit at the hands of Aberdeen, followed by a 3-1 reversal at home to Rangers, when the champions turned on the style. The Hearts board reacted, some felt hastily, by dismissing MacDonald and putting Sandy Clark in charge on an interim basis. While Clark was taking charge of Hearts at the Ukrainian outpost of Dnepropetrovsk, it was revealed that Joe Jordan, rated one of the brightest young managers in the British game, would be the new manager. It took him time to put his mark on the team. Hearts lost to Airdrie in the third round of the Scottish Cup in January and the final league placing of fifth was two places below the previous year.

Nevertheless, Jordan was moulding a team that was difficult to beat and, in 1991-92, Hearts won their first six matches and hit a rich vein of form at the end of the year, as they put together a run of 15 unbeaten matches, culminating in a thrilling 2-1 win over Celtic at Parkhead in early January to head the league. But just when there was talk that this could be Hearts' year, there was a crushing 4-0 home defeat by Aberdeen the week after the Parkhead victory, which removed Hearts from their perch. The following week, Hearts slipped to a 1-0 defeat at Airdrie who, managed by Alex MacDonald, were becoming something of a nuisance to Jordan and Hearts. In the Scottish Cup semi finals, Hearts could not beat MacDonald's side in two matches and eventually lost in a 'penalty shoot-out' - the club's fourth successive defeat in a major semi final. So Hearts finished runners-up again in the league and fell at the penultimate hurdle in the cup but there was a feeling that, had Jordan been given more money to invest in the squad when they were top of the league - there was little cover for Gary Mackay and Tosh McKinlay in the demanding wing-back roles - then the trophy famine could have ended.

Hearts missed out on a European place the following season when they could only finish fifth in the league and there was also what was becoming the perennial Scottish Cup semi final defeat - this time 2-1 at the hands of Rangers. It was clear all was not well when Hearts were humiliated 6-0 by Falkirk at Brockville - their biggest defeat since an identical scoreline against

Celtic at Celtic Park on April 1, 1981. Jordan was dismissed a couple of days after this result and was replaced by Sandy Clark, who had been responsible for bringing through much of the new young talent at the club, like Gary Locke, Allan Johnston and Kevin Thomas. Clark had a difficult season and Hearts managed only 11 league wins in 44 matches, although there was a memorable 2-1 Scottish Cup fourth round win over Hibs at Easter Road before Rangers ended the cup interest in the following round. Hearts had to go to the final day in the league as reconstruction meant three teams were to be relegated and only a nervy 1-0 win over Partick Thistle at Firhill, when Alan McLaren scored the winning goal, kept them up.

Clark, and his assistant Hugh McCann, were to fall victim to a change of ownership in the club when Chris Robinson, head of a catering firm, and solicitor Leslie Deans bought out Mercer for £2.1 million. *"This is a happy end to a long journey,"* Robinson stated at the takeover. *"Les and I are confident we can take Hearts forward into a new and exciting era. We can't promise success on the field but clearly one of our ambitions is to see Hearts win a trophy."*

The new owners immediately installed Tommy McLean, who had an admirable track record on a limited budget at Motherwell, as manager. More change to the playing personnel followed and, with such upheaval on and off the field of play, it was not surprising that it was another inconsistent season. It had started badly, with defenders Craig Levein and Graeme Hogg sent off for fighting each other in a pre-season friendly at Raith Rovers. Both were given lengthy SFA bans following club fines. Hogg did not play for the club again, being offloaded to Notts County. Hearts also surrendered their long unbeaten streak – which had stretched to 22 matches - against arch-rivals, Hibs, when Gordon Hunter scored the only goal of an early-season encounter at Tynecastle.

It was another difficult season - gifted defender, Alan McLaren, finally departed for Rangers to help ease the financial situation and Airdrie again bundled Hearts out of the Scottish Cup at the semi-final stage, when Steve Cooper scored in a 1-0 win for Alex MacDonald's side. Hearts again flirted with relegation but Brian Hamilton and John Robertson scored in a 2-0 'home' win over Motherwell in the final match, which meant the club avoided a relegation play-off. McLean was dismissed not long after the end of the season when it was obvious relationships with the board were strained. McLean took the club to court, alleging unfair dismissal and the matter was later settled out of court. Hearts had to turn over a new page and by turning to former player, Jim Jefferies, as their next manager, a significant chapter in the club's history was about to begin.

A SILVER FINISH

JIM JEFFERIES had experienced the highs and lows of a Tynecastle playing career in the seventies and, if he had become a manager more by accident than design, it had been clear for some time that this was his vocation.

Having started with lowly Lauder, in the Borders Amateur League, he had served his apprenticeship through Hawick Royal Albert, Gala Fairydean, Berwick and Falkirk. Jefferies was working in the insurance business when the call came from his local club in 1985-86 and he hoisted them from second bottom of the amateur league to fourth top within a matter of months.

"Jim was reluctant to give the commitment until he had met the players first," recalls George Kerr, Jefferies' predecessor at Lauder and possibly the man most responsible for cajoling Jefferies into management. *"When he met the players, he told them that all he required of them was to give of their time twice a week for training and on a Saturday for matches. If they could not do that, then he did not want them. What he was effectively telling them was that if he was giving the commitment, then he expected them to do the same."*

Jefferies admits that he made mistakes when he was learning his trade but it was away from the glare that a Premier Division manager is subjected to. After seeing what he achieved at Falkirk, Chris Robinson and Leslie Deans were convinced Jefferies was the man to take Hearts to the next level and did not take 'no' for an answer when it seemed as if Jefferies had made a u-turn on his decision to manage the club after an ill-advised meeting with Falkirk chairman, George Fulston. Fulston emerged from that Saturday meeting and announced that his manager had agreed to stay but, even on the drive back to Lauder, Jefferies suspected he was turning down the job he had always craved and was destined for.

Robinson and Deans were still convinced that the lure of a Tynecastle return would be too great and, even by the Monday, it was clear Jefferies was about to make another dramatic u-turn. The decision to pursue him, even when all had seemed lost, is unquestionably the most important decision the new Hearts board have taken. Billy Brown, Jefferies' assistant at Falkirk, was also part of the equation and both were given five-year contracts and the promise of time to turn the club around.

It was obvious from the outset that Jefferies would bring a touch of wizardry. Watching his first game at Derby's Baseball Ground, when he left Eamonn Bannon to continue with team duties in a pre-season friendly, he saw his new charges torn apart 3-0 by half-time. He left his seat in the stand for a few words with the players at half-time and, by the full-time whistle, Hearts had rewarded their vociferous travelling band of supporters with a 3-3 draw.

It was a start that showed Hearts up for what they were at the time - fearless but flawed. Jefferies was to dismantle the team and rebuild it almost from scratch in the months ahead. The enormity of the task that faced the new manager became apparent by the autumn, when Hearts slumped to the bottom of the league and 2-0 defeat by his former club, Falkirk, at Brockville. David Weir, later to flourish at Tynecastle, scored one of the goals, and the match convinced Jefferies that 'Hearts-surgery' was becoming critical.

Goalkeeper Henry Smith had already been replaced after he surrendered four goals in a Coca-Cola Cup exit at Dundee and, when Craig Nelson and Gary O'Connor had not filled the gloves convincingly enough to suggest they were the long-term answer, Jefferies used all his acumen on the transfer market to bring in former French international goalkeeper, Gilles Rousset. Rousset played in the defeat at Brockville but looked very capable and his influence over the months ahead was to prove important.

The manager did not stop there - a Swedish striker, Hans Eskilsson, came in and an Italian defender, Pasquale Bruno, who had a fearsome reputation which had made him infamous in Italy. But he had played in two European finals and had the character to take Hearts by the scruff of their necks. Neil Pointon, an experienced English defender, also came in and midfield player Steve Fulton, who was burdened in his early days at Celtic Park by his former manager comparing him to Roberto Baggio, was also signed. Just as important, Jefferies was showing a willingness to open the door to the youth of Tynecastle and was not afraid to give players like Gary Locke, Paul Ritchie, Allan Johnston and Alan McManus their chance. Locke, indeed, was to be made captain as the new Hearts took shape.

The league was obviously outwith reach but the ambitious Jefferies had set his sights on silverware in his first season. The Scottish Cup was the only available trophy and, for once, Hearts successfully negotiated the penultimate obstacle, beating Aberdeen in a dramatic semi final, with a late goal from Johnston, moments after Duncan Shearer had equalised a John Robertson goal. Since reaching the Cup Final in 1986, Hearts had lost no fewer than six semi finals under three different managers (five in the Scottish Cup and one in the League Cup). In fact, Hearts' semi-final record stretching back to 1977 was abysmal, with only one win in eleven before 1996 (in 1986, against Dundee United).

Any game-plan that Jefferies had been considering in the final against Rangers was wiped out within minutes, as Locke suffered a freak knee injury in the eighth minute when his studs caught in the turf. It was an injury that was to put him out of action for the best part of a year. Trailing to a Brian Laudrup goal at half-time did not seem too much of a hill to climb but hopes deteriorated considerably shortly after the restart when another Laudrup shot slipped through Rousset's grasp and, in that moment, the cup also slipped through Hearts' fingers. Aided and abetted by Laudrup, Gordon Durie went on to score a 'hat-trick' and Hearts' only consolation in a 5-1 defeat was the distant John Colquhoun shot which brought the goal. More construction work needed to be done in the close-season by Jefferies.

He brought in David Weir and Neil McCann from Falkirk and Dundee respectively and also former Norwich midfield player, Jeremy Goss, a full Welsh international cap. Within a matter of months, Hearts were back in a cup final - the Coca-Cola Cup, again against Rangers - and this time it was to be the magic of Paul Gascoigne that denied them silverware. Hearts trailed 2-0 but, with McCann stamping his class on the final, had pulled level through goals from Steve Fulton and John Robertson. There was also a controversial refereeing decision when Robertson looked to be impeded by Joachim Bjorklund but play was allowed to continue and Gascoigne went on to score. He notched his second shortly afterwards and suddenly 2-2 had become 2-4. Weir headed a late goal for Hearts but an equaliser was not forthcoming and so another final was lost, this time 4-3. But there was a feeling that Hearts were getting closer.

Dundee United ended Scottish Cup aspirations that season when Robbie Winters scored the only goal of a fourth-round replay at Tannadice and, while Hearts improved to fourth in the league, it was an inconsistent season, with points dropped against teams at the lower end of the table.

More signings followed in the summer of 1997, as Jefferies again spread the net wide to bring in Austrian cap, Thomas Flogel and French striker, Stephane Adam, from Metz. With French striker, Stephane Paille, having returned home in disgrace at the end of the previous season after a drugs scandal, Hearts were still trying to find the right permutation up front. Although John Robertson was being used sparingly, he was still finding the net with regularity but he could not go on forever. Jim Hamilton had looked the part when he came into the side and Adam was also to make a telling impact as the new season unfolded.

Indeed, Adam was to achieve what Robertson had failed to do in his career, namely score a Premier Division 'hat-trick', when he made his mark in a pulsating 5-3 league win over Kilmarnock at Tynecastle in the November.

What Jefferies possessed was variety in attack - Flogel and McCann could also be pushed into central striking roles on occasion - and, with the seemingly tireless Colin Cameron and the creative Steve Fulton also having an eye for goal, there was a goal threat from throughout the Hearts team.

Jose Quitongo, a gifted and effervescent Angolan, was added during the season and a late equaliser against Celtic in a crucial league match at Tynecastle quickly endeared him to the home supporters.

Unfortunately for Hearts, there was an early Coca-Cola Cup exit at the hands of Dunfermline at East End Park in a tie where the visitors were dominant but it was only to make Hearts more determined as they pursued silver on two fronts, the league and the Scottish Cup. With many people under the misconception that it would be a straight fight between Rangers and Celtic for the league, Hearts took the race to the closing weeks of the season. Remarkably, Hearts lasted the course in spite of the fact that they failed to beat either of the 'Old Firm' in eight league matches. Their consistency against the other seven teams was breathtaking - 15 goals were scored in four matches against Aberdeen, only one goal was lost in four matches against Dundee United and, outside of the 'Old Firm', only Dunfermline and Hibs managed to beat Hearts and eight months separated those defeats.

Hearts put together a run of 17 league and cup matches without defeat before Hibs dented their title hopes in the April by taking all three points in a match they needed to win to keep alive their hopes of avoiding relegation. But if Hearts faltered at the end of a punishing league chase (only one win in their last seven league matches), the cup run had been gathering momentum.

It had been rather straightforward from the outset, with the draw being kind to Hearts. Three 'home' draws against lower division opposition is much more than you are entitled to expect from a cup competition but Hearts went about their progress to the semi final with diligence, beating Clydebank 2-0, Albion Rovers 3-0 and Ayr United 4-1, before travelling to Ibrox to face Falkirk, another lower division side, in the semi finals after providence smiled on them again and paired Rangers and Celtic in the other semi final.

But Falkirk, having beaten Celtic the previous year and under the experienced Alex Totten, were no mean opponents. Adam scored early enough but Kevin McAllister's late equaliser looked set to take it to a replay, until even later goals from McCann and Adam put Hearts through to their third domestic final under Jim Jefferies in three seasons. The odds of a final win, at last, were tumbling.

Jefferies prepared his team meticulously. He took his players to Stratford, where Scotland had prepared for the 1996 European Championships and it was in these pampered surroundings that the game plan was written. Jefferies has observed that Hearts had lost 13 goals in their four league meetings with Rangers that season and knew that this time he could not afford to throw caution to the wind and hit Rangers with an all-out assault. Hearts needed to be more careful with their distribution, more guarded in defence and shut down the midfield. Without the menace of Paul Gascoigne, he knew Rangers' match-winning options were limited but there was still the considerable threat of Brian Laudrup and the predatory Ally McCoist. Most worryingly, Rangers had just given up their league title to Celtic and wanted to avoid a trophyless season in Walter Smith's last year as manager.

Unhappily, it was confirmed in the days before the final that the unlucky Locke would again miss out due to injury but Jefferies was still confident he had the players capable of giving Hearts their first silver in 36 years. Steve Fulton was informed that he would be captain and bleached his hair for the occasion and, as the Hearts players disembarked from their coach at Celtic Park, there was a belief that they could make history. The jibe before the final that the club had never won anything "in colour" was quickly to be forgotten. The Hearts supporters had snapped up every available ticket to give a maroon backdrop to the final as the team took the field.

Twenty-two years previously, Hearts had lost a goal to Rangers in a final after less than a minute and it was recorded that referee Bobby Davidson started the match a minute early. So, technically, Hearts were a goal down before kick-off time. Jefferies had played in that final and must have warned his players about the dangers of losing concentration so early in a final. As fate would have it, it was Hearts who were given the chance to score after just half-a-minute, when referee, Willie Young, adjudged that Fulton was brought down inches inside the penalty area by Sergio Porrini.

Colin Cameron had demonstrated earlier in the season - against St Johnstone at Tynecastle, when Hearts were awarded a penalty in injury-time - that he had the nerve and he calmly swept the ball into the roof of the net. The midfield player, who had been a doubt in the weeks before the final with a pelvic injury, later revealed that he changed his mind which way he would place the ball during his approach, something penalty takers always advise against, but it worked out well. As the Hearts fans settled after celebrating the goal, the question was whether it had come too early, something Jefferies admitted afterwards that he had feared.

Predictably, Rangers came back but Hearts shut down the space between the ball and their goal and when Rangers did look like penetrating the most disciplined of defences, Rousset was there to make amends for his lapse two years previously. He handled crosses immaculately, showed lightning reflexes when required and deservedly won the 'Man of the Match' award. If most of the play was in Hearts' half, then clear-cut chances were scarce and when Adam pounced on a mistake by Lorenzo Amoruso nine minutes into the second half to put Hearts two ahead, even the most battle weary of the Hearts supporters must have felt that this could finally be the year.

But it was never going to be a comfortable ending. Ally McCoist, brought into the fray at half-time, pulled a goal back with a precise shot in the 81st minute and suddenly Rangers saw their chance of taking the match to extra time and producing another cruel 'Heart-breaker'. McCoist was clear again when Weir tripped him on the edge of the penalty-area. It appeared as if referee Young had pointed to the spot as Celtic Park held its breath. But, no. He gave a free-kick just an inch outside the area and Hearts held firm.

Manager Jefferies admitted that the final few minutes were the longest in his life, as Rangers attempted to go for the jugular but, for once, Hearts were not to be denied. The only slight disappointment was that amidst all the frantic defending, John Robertson was not able to get on the pitch to play some small part in the final triumph. Jefferies fully intended to bring him on but it was all hands to the pumps in injury time.

Celtic Park has never known such a 'Jambo-ree' at the final whistle, though some fans were still stunned that the waiting for a trophy was finally over. Not that they had come expecting defeat but rather they had learned through the years not to take anything for granted. It took more than three blasts of Mr Young's whistle to convince them.

Locke joined Fulton on the pitch and the duo hoisted the Scottish Cup together, a moment Locke will treasure forever. He was almost prevented from joining the team in their victory celebrations on the pitch due to some petty officialdom but the maroon banners were to cut through the red tape.

Estimates of the crowd awaiting Hearts at Tynecastle that evening vary but 20,000 seemed conservative. As the team coach approached Edinburgh on the M8, fans were out on the motorway bridges cheering the team home for their victory celebrations. The following day, as many as 250,000 lined the streets of the capital as the open-top bus made its way through Haymarket to Gorgie, where a capacity crowd awaited at Tynecastle to greet the team. The fans literally shouted from the rooftops.

When it had all sunk in, there was the feeling that this is only the start. St Mirren, Dundee United and Hibernian had all won silverware in the recent past and yet been relegated within a few seasons, so there is no danger of any complacency creeping in. But Hearts have a tendency to win trophies in clusters. The team won six in 16 years between 1891-1906 and then seven in nine years between 1954-62 and have never won a cup in isolation. As chief executive Robinson remarked: *"The future's bright, the future's maroon."*

Just four days after the Cup Final win, Hearts won the BP Youth Cup at Tynecastle to show that there is reason to be optimistic about the future. Gary Naysmith, Grant Murray, Roddy McKenzie, David Murie, Derek Holmes and Kris O'Neil have all been pushing first-team claims in the knowledge that Jefferies will give youth a chance. Not content to rest on the laurels, Rob McKinnon has signed from FC Twente and Steven Pressley has joined from Dundee United and both believe they can win honours at Tynecastle. Hearts are approaching the turn of the century with as much anticipation as they did a hundred years ago.

HEARTS' RECORD: THE FACTS

Scottish Cup progress:

1875-76: First round: Drew twice with 3rd Edinburgh Rifle Volunteers.
Both clubs progressed to second round.
Second round: lost 2-0 Drumpellier.

1876-77: First round: scratched to Dunfermline.

1877-78: First round: lost 2-1 Hibernian.

1878-79: First round: bt Swifts 3-1.
Second round: bt Thistle 1-0.
Third round: bt Arbroath 2-1.
Fourth round: scratched to Helensburgh.

1879-80: First round: walkover (3rd ERV scratched).
Second round: bt Brunswick 3-2.
Third round: lost 2-1 Hibernian.

1880-81: First round: bt Brunswick 3-1.
Second round: bye.
Third round: bt Hibernian 5-3.
Fourth round: bt Cambuslang 3-0.
Fifth round: lost 4-0 Arthurlie.

1881-82: First round: lost 1-2 St Bernards.

1882-83: First round: bt St Bernards 4-3 (after draw).
Second round: bt Addiewell 14-0.
Third round: lost 8-1 Vale of Leven.

1883-84: First round: bt Brunswick 8-0.
Second round: bt Newcastleton 4-1.
Third round: lost 4-1 Hibernian.

1884-85: First round: bye.
Second round: Expelled on protest of Dunfermline.

1885-86: First round: bt St Bernards 1-0 (after protested game).
Second round: lost 2-1 Hibernian.

1886-87: First round: bt Edina 7-1.
Second round: bt Broxburn Thistle 2-1.
Third round: lost 5-1 Hibernian.

1887-88: First round: bt Norton Park 4-1.
Second round: bye.
Third round: bt Hibernian 3-1 (after 1-1 draw).
Fourth round: lost 4-2 St Mirren (after 1-1, 2-2 and 2-2 draws).

1888-89: First round: bt Bo'ness 1-0.
Second round: bt Erin Rovers 7-0.
Third round: bt Broxburn 2-0 (after 2-2 draw).
Fourth round: lost 3-1 Campsie.

1889-90: First round: bt St Bernards 3-0.
Second round: bt Bellstane Birds 4-1.
Third round: bt Champfleurie 5-0.
Fourth round: bt Alloa 9-1.
Fifth round: lost 3-1 Vale of Leven.

1890-91: First round: bt Raith Rovers 7-2.
Second round: walkover (Burntisland scratched).
Third round: bt Methlan Park 3-0.
Fourth round: bt Ayr 4-3.
Fifth round: bt Morton 5-1.
Sixth round: bt East Stirling 3-1.
Semi-final: bt Third Lanark 4-1.
Final: bt Dumbarton 1-0.

1891-92: First round: bt Clyde 8-0 (after protested game)
Second round: bt Broxburn Shamrock 5-4.
Third round: lost 3-2 Renton (after 4-4 and 2-2 draws).

1892-93: First round: bt Stenhousemuir 8-0 (after 1-1 draw).

Second round: bt Motherwell 4-2.

Third round: lost 5-1 Queen's Park (after 1-1 draw).

1893-94: First round: lost 1-0 St Mirren.

1894-95: First round: bt Rangers 2-1.

Second round: bt Abercorn 6-1.

Third round: bt King's Park 4-2.

Semi-final: lost 1-0 St Bernards (after 0-0 draw).

1895-96: First round: bt Blantyre 12-1.

Second round: bt Ayr 5-1.

Third round: bt Arbroath 4-0.

Fourth round: bt St Bernards 1-0.

Final: bt Hibernian 3-1.

1896-97: First round: bt Clyde 2-0.

Second round: lost 5-2 Third Lanark.

1897-98: First round: bt Lochee United 8-0.

Second round: bt Morton 4-1.

Third round: lost 3-0 Dundee.

1898-99: First round: lost 4-1 Rangers.

1899-1900: First round: bt St Mirren 3-0 (after 0-0 draw).

Second round: bt Hibernian 2-1 (after 1-1 draw).

Third round: bt Third Lanark 2-1.

Semi-final: lost 2-1 Queen's Park.

1900-01: First round: bt Mossend Swifts 7-0.

Second round: bt Queen's Park 2-1.

Third round: bt Port Glasgow 5-1.

Semi-final: bt Hibernian 2-1 (after 1-1 draw).

Final: bt Celtic 4-3.

1901-02: First round: bt Cowdenbeath 3-0 (after 0-0 draw).

Second round: bt Third Lanark 4-1.

Third round: lost 2-1 Celtic (after 1-1 draw).

1902-03: First round: bt Clyde 2-1.

Second round: bt Ayr 4-2.

Third round: bt Third Lanark 2-1.

Semi-final: bt Dundee 1-0 (after 0-0 draw).

Final: lost 0-2 Rangers (after 1-1 and 0-0 draws).

1903-04: First round: lost 3-2 Rangers.

1904-05: First round: bt Dundee 3-1.

Second round: lost 2-1 St Mirren.

1905-06: First round: bt Nithsdale Wanderers 4-1.

Second round: bt Beith 3-0.

Third round: bt Celtic 2-1.

Semi-final: bt Port Glasgow 2-0.

Final: bt Third Lanark 1-0.

1906-07: First round: bt Airdrie 2-0 (after 0-0 draw).

Second round: bt Kilmarnock 2-1 (after 0-0 draw).

Third round: bt Raith Rovers 1-0 (after 2-2 draw).

Semi-final: bt Queen's Park 1-0.

Final: lost 3-0 Celtic.

1907-08: First round: bt St Johnstone 4-1.

Second round: bt Port Glasgow 4-0.

Third round: lost 3-1 St Mirren (after abandoned game).

1908-09: First round: bt Kilmarnock 2-1.

Second round: lost Airdrie 2-0.

1908-09: First Round: bt Kilmarnock 2-1.

Second round: lost 2-0 Airdrie.

1909-10: First round: bt Bathgate 4-0.

Second round: bt St Mirren 4-0 (after 2-2 and 0-0 draws).

Third round: lost 1-0 Hibernian (after abandoned game).

1910-11: First round: lost 1-0 Clyde (after 1-1 draw).

1911-12: First round: bt Hibernian 3-1 (after 0-0, 1-1 (abandoned) and 1-1 draws).
Second round: bt Dundee 1-0.
Third round: bt Morton 1-0.
Semi-final: lost 3-0 Celtic.

1912-13: First round: bye.
Second round: bt Dunfermline 3-1.
Third round: bt Kilmarnock 2-0.
Fourth round: bt Celtic 1-0.
Semi-final: lost 1-0 Falkirk.

1913-14: First round: bye.
Second round: lost 2-0 Raith Rovers.

1914-18: Competition suspended.

1919-20: First round: bt Nithsdale Wanderers 5-1.
Second round: bt Falkirk 2-0.
Third round: lost 1-0 Aberdeen.

1920-21: First round: bye.
Second round: bt Clyde 3-2 (after 1-1 and 0-0 draws).
Third round: bt Hamilton Academical 1-0.
Fourth round: bt Celtic 2-1.
Semi-final: lost 2-0 Partick Thistle (after two 0-0 draws).

1921-22: First round: bt Arthurlie 2-1.
Second round: bt Broxburn 3-1 (after two 2-2 draws).
Third round: lost 4-0 Rangers.

1922-23: First round: bt Thornhill 6-0.
Second round: lost 3-2 Bo'ness.

1923-24: First round: bt Third Lanark 3-0 (after 0-0 draw).
Second round: bt Galston 6-0.
Third round: bt Clyde 3-1.
Fourth round: lost 2-1 Falkirk.

1924-25: First round: bt Leith Athletic 4-1.

Second round: lost 2-1 Kilmarnock.

1925-26: First round: bt Dundee United 6-0 (after 1-1 draw).

Second round: bt Alloa 5-2.

Third round: lost 4-0 Celtic.

1926-27: First round: lost 3-2 Clyde.

1927-28: First round: bt St Johnstone 1-0 (after 2-2 draw).

Second round: bt Forres Mechanics 7-0.

Third round: lost 2-1 Motherwell.

1928-29: First round: lost 2-0 Airdrie.

1929-30: First round: bt Clydebank 1-0.

Second round: bt St Bernards 5-0 (after 0-0 draw).

Third round: bt Hibernian 3-1.

Fourth round: bt Dundee 4-0 (after 2-2 draw).

Semi-final: lost 4-1 Rangers.

1930-31: First round: bt Stenhousemuir 9-1.

Second round: lost 3-2 Kilmarnock.

1931-32: First round: bt Lochgelly 13-3.

Second round: bt Cowdenbeath 4-1.

Third round: lost 1-0 Rangers.

1932-33: First round: bt Solway Star 3-0.

Second round: bt Airdrie 6-0.

Third round: bt St Johnstone 2-0.

Fourth round: bt Hibernian 2-0 (after 0-0 draw).

Fifth round: lost 2-1 Celtic (after 0-0 draw).

1933-34: First round: bt Montrose 5-1.

Second round: bt Queen's Park 2-1.

Third round: lost 2-1 Rangers (after 0-0 draw).

1934-35: First round: bt Solway Star 7-0.
Second round: bt Kilmarnock 2-0.
Third round: bt Dundee United 4-2 (after 2-2 draw).
Fourth round: bt Airdrie 3-2.
Semi-final: lost 2-0 Rangers (after 1-1 draw).

1935-36: First round: lost 2-0 Third Lanark.

1936-37: First round: bt St Bernards 3-1.
Second round: bt King's Park 15-0.
Third round: lost 2-1 Hamilton Academicals.

1937-38: First round: lost 3-1 Dundee United.

1938-39: First round: bt Penicuik Athletic 14-2.
Second round: bt Elgin City 14-1.
Third round: lost 2-1 Celtic (after 2-2 draw).

1939-40: First round: bt St Johnstone 4-2 (after 2-2 draw).
Second round: bt Raith Rovers 2-1.
Third round: lost 4-3 Airdrie (after 0-0 and 2-2 draws).

1940-45: Competition suspended.

1946-47: First round: bt St Johnstone 3-0.
Second round: bye.
Third round: bt Cowdenbeath 2-0.
Fourth round: lost 2-1 Arbroath.

1947-48: First round: bt Dundee 4-2.
Second round: lost 2-1 Airdrie.

1948-49: First round: bt Airdrie 4-1.
Second round: bt Third Lanark 4-1.
Third round: bt Dumbarton 3-0.
Fourth round: lost 4-2 Dundee.

1949-50: First round: bt Dundee 2-1 (after 1-1 draw).
Second round: lost 3-1 Aberdeen.

1950-51: First round: bt Alloa 3-2.

Second round: bt East Stirling 5-1.

Third round: lost 2-1 Celtic.

1951-52: First round: bye.

Second round: bt Raith Rovers 1-0.

Third round: bt Queen of the South 3-1.

Fourth round: bt Airdrie 6-4 (after 2-2 draw).

Semi-final:lost 3-1 Motherwell (after two 1-1 draws).

1952-53: First round: bye.

Second round: bt Raith Rovers 1-0.

Third round: bt Montrose 2-1.

Fourth round: bt Queen of the South 2-1.

Semi-final: lost 2-1 Rangers.

1953-54: First round: bye.

Second round: bt Fraserburgh 3-0.

Third round: bt Queen of the South 2-1.

Fourth round: lost 4-0 Aberdeen.

1954-55: First round: bt Hibernian 5-0.

Second round: bt Buckie Thistle 6-0.

Third round: lost 2-1 Aberdeen (after 1-1 draw).

1955-56: First round: bt Forfar 3-0.

Second round: bt Stirling Albion 5-0.

Third round: bt Rangers 4-0.

Semi-final: bt Raith Rovers 3-0.

Final: bt Celtic 3-1.

1956-57: First round: lost 4-0 Rangers.

1957-58: First round: bt East Fife 2-1.

Second round: bt Albion Rovers 4-1.

Third round: lost 4-3 Hibernian.

1958-59: First round: bt Queen of the South 3-1.

Second round: lost 3-2 Rangers.

1959-60: First round: lost 2-1 Kilmarnock (after 1-1 draw).

1960-61: First round: bt Tarff Rovers 9-0.
Second round: bt Kilmarnock 2-1.
Third round: bt Partick Thistle 2-1.
Fourth round: lost 1-0 St Mirren.

1961-62: First round: bye.
Second round: bt Vale of Leithen 5-0.
Third round: lost 4-3 Celtic.

1962-63: First round: bt Forfar 3-1.
Second round: lost 3-1 Celtic.

1963-64: First round: bye.
Second round: bt Queen of the South 3-0.
Third round: lost 2-1 Motherwell (after 3-3 draw).

1964-65: First round: bt Falkirk 3-0.
Second round: bt Morton 2-0 (after 3-3 draw).
Third round: lost 1-0 Motherwell.

1965-66: First round: bt Clyde 2-1.
Second round: bt Hibernian 2-1.
Third round: lost 3-1 Celtic (after 3-3 draw).

1966-67: First round: lost 3-0 Dundee United.

1967-68: First round: bt Brechin City 4-1.
Second round: bt Dundee United 6-5.
Third round: bt Rangers 1-0 (after 1-1 draw).
Semi-final: bt Morton 2-1 (after 1-1 draw).
Final: lost 3-1 Dunfermline.

1968-69: First round: bt Dundee 2-1.
Second round: lost 2-0 Rangers.

1969-70: First round: bt Montrose 1-0 (after 1-1 draw).
Second round: lost 2-0 Kilmarnock.

1970-71: First round: bt Stranraer 3-0.

Second round: lost 2-1 Hibernian.

1971-72: First round: bt St Johnstone 2-0.

Second round: bt Clydebank 4-0.

Third round: lost 1-0 Celtic (after 1-1 draw).

1972-73: First round: lost 3-1 Airdrie (after 0-0 draw).

1973-74: Third round: bt Clyde 3-1.

Fourth round: bt Partick Thistle 4-1 (after 1-1 draw).

Fifth round: bt Ayr United 2-1 (after 1-1 draw).

Semi-final: lost 4-2 Dundee United (after 1-1 draw).

1974-75: Third round: bt Kilmarnock 2-0.

Fourth round: bt Queen of the South 2-0.

Fifth round: lost 3-2 Dundee (after 1-1 draw).

1975-76: Third round: bt Clyde 1-0 (after 2-2 draw).

Fourth round: bt Stirling Albion 4-0.

Fifth round: bt Montrose 2-1 (after two 2-2 draws).

Semi-final: bt Dumbarton 3-0 (after 0-0 draw).

Final: lost 3-1 Rangers.

1976-77: Third round: bt Dumbarton 1-0 (after 1-1 draw).

Fourth round: bt Clydebank 1-0.

Fifth round: bt East Fife 3-2 (after 0-0 draw).

Semi-final: lost 2-0 Rangers.

1977-78: Third round: bt Airdrie 3-2.

Fourth round: lost 1-0 Dumbarton (after 1-1 draw).

1978-79: Third round: bt Raith Rovers 2-0.

Fourth round: bt Morton 1-0 (after 1-1 draw).

Fifth round: lost 2-1 Hibernian.

1979-80: Third round: bt Alloa 1-0.

Fourth round: bt Stirling Albion 2-0.

Fifth round: lost 6-1 Rangers.

1980-81: Third round: lost 3-1 Morton (after 0-0 draw).

1981-82: Third round: bt East Stirling 4-1.
Fourth round: lost 1-0 Forfar.

1982-83: Third round: bt Queen of the South 1-0 (after 1-1 draw).
Fourth round: bt East Fife 2-1.
Fifth round: lost 4-1 Celtic.

1983-84: Third round: bt Partick Thistle 2-0.
Fourth round: lost 2-1 Dundee United.

1984-85: Third round: bt Inverness Caley 6-0.
Fourth round: bt Brechin City 1-0 (after 1-1 draw).
Fifth round : lost 1-0 Aberdeen (after 1-1 draw).

1985-86: Third round: bt Rangers 3-2.
Fourth round: bt Hamilton Academicals 2-1.
Fifth round: bt St Mirren 4-1.
Semi-final: bt Dundee United 1-0.
Final: lost 3-0 Aberdeen.

1986-87: Third round: bt Kilmarnock 3-1 (after 0-0 and 1-1 draws).
Fourth round: bt Celtic 1-0.
Fifth round: bt Motherwell 1-0 (after 1-1 draw).
Semi-final: lost 2-1 St Mirren.

1987-88: Third round: bt Falkirk 3-1.
Fourth round: bt Morton 2-0.
Fifth round: bt Dunfermline 3-0.
Semi-final: lost Celtic 2-1.

1988-89: Third round: bt Ayr United 4-1.
Fourth round: bt Partick Thistle 2-0.
Fifth round: lost Celtic 2-1.

1989-90: Third round: bt Falkirk 2-0.
Fourth round: bt Motherwell 4-0.
Fifth round: lost 4-1 Aberdeen.

1990-91: Third round: lost 2-1 Airdrie.

1991-92: Third round: bt St Mirren 3-0 (after 0-0 draw).
Fourth round: bt Dunfermline 2-1.
Fifth round: bt Falkirk 3-1.
Semi-final: lost 4-2 on penalties Airdrie (after 0-0 and 1-1 draws).

1992-93: Third round: bt Huntly 6-0.
Fourth round: bt Dundee 2-0.
Fifth round: bt Falkirk 2-0.
Semi-final: lost 2-1 Rangers.

1993-94: Third round: bt Partick Thistle 1-0.
Fourth round: bt Hibernian 2-1.
Fifth round: lost 2-0 Rangers.

1994-95: Third round: bt Clydebank 2-1 (after 1-1 draw).
Fourth round: bt Rangers 4-2.
Fifth round: bt Dundee United 2-0.
Semi-final: lost 1-0 Airdrie.

1995-96: Third round: bt Partick Thistle 1-0.
Fourth round: bt Kilmarnock 2-1.
Fifth round: bt St Johnstone 2-1.
Semi-final: bt Aberdeen 2-1.
Final: lost 5-1 Rangers.

1996-97: Third round: bt Cowdenbeath 5-0.
Fourth round: lost 1-0 Dundee United (after 1-1 draw).

1997-98: Third round: bt Clydebank 2-0.
Fourth round: bt Albion Rovers 3-0.
Fifth round: bt Ayr United 4-1.
Semi-final: bt Falkirk 2-1.
Final: bt Rangers 2-1.

League Cup progress:

1946-47: Qualifying round: Clyde 2-1, 2-1; Kilmarnock 3-1, 0-2; Partick Thistle 4-4, 1-1.
Quarter-final: East Fife 0-1, 5-2.
Semi-final: Aberdeen 2-6.

1947-48: Qualifying round: Airdrie 2-3, 1-0; Hibernian 2-1, 2-1; Clyde 1-0, 2-5.
Quarter-final: East Fife 3-4.

1948-49: Qualifying round: Partick Thistle 2-2, 1-3; East Fife 0-4, 6-1;
Queen of the South 3-2, 4-0.

1949-50: Qualifying round: Stirling Albion 5-1, 4-5; Raith Rovers 5-1, 2-1; East Fife 1-1, 3-4.

1950-51: Qualifying round: Partick Thistle 1-1, 2-0; Motherwell 4-1, 2-3; Airdrie 3-2, 3-1.

1951-52: Qualifying round: Raith Rovers 1-0, 0-2; Dundee 1-2, 5-2; St Mirren 5-1, 3-1.

1952-53: Qualifying round: Rangers 5-0, 0-2; Aberdeen 4-2, 1-1; Motherwell 0-1, 2-1.

1953-54: Qualifying round: Hamilton 5-0, 1-1; Rangers 1-4, 1-1; Raith Rovers 2-0, 1-3.

1954-55: Qualifying round: Dundee 3-1, 1-4; Falkirk 6-2 4-1; Celtic 2-1, 3-2.
Quarter-final: St Johnstone 5-0, 2-0.
Semi-final: Airdrie 4-1.
Final: bt Motherwell 4-2.

1955-56: Qualifying round: Partick Thistle 2-0, 2-1; Raith Rovers 5-0, 2-0; East Fife 0-1, 4-0.
Quarter-final: Aberdeen 3-5, 2-4.

1956-57: Qualifying round: Hibernian 6-1, 2-1; Partick Thistle 1-3, 2-2; Falkirk 5-0, 1-1.

1957-58: Qualifying round: Kilmarnock 1-2, 1-1; Queen's Park 9-2, 0-0;
Dundee 2-2 (after abandoned match), 4-2.

1958-59: Qualifying round: Rangers 0-3, 2-1; Third Lanark 3-0, 5-4; Raith Rovers 3-1, 3-1.
Quarter-final: Ayr United 5-1, 3-1.
Semi-final: Kilmarnock 3-0.
Final: bt Partick Thistle 5-1.

1959-60: Qualifying round: Kilmarnock 4-0, 2-0; Aberdeen 2-2, 4-1; Stirling Albion 2-1, 2-2.

Quarter-final: Motherwell 1-1, 6-2.

Semi-final: Cowdenbeath 9-3.

Final: bt Third Lanark 2-1.

1960-61: Qualifying round: St Mirren 1-1, 1-3; Clyde 0-2, 6-2; Motherwell 3-2, 2-1;
Clyde (play-off) 1-2.

1961-62: Qualifying round: Raith Rovers 1-0, 1-3; Kilmarnock 2-1, 2-0; St Mirren 0-1, 3-1.

Quarter-final: Hamilton 2-1, 2-0.

Semi-final: Stirling Albion 2-1.

Final: lost 3-1 Rangers (after 1-1 draw).

1962-63: Qualifying round: Celtic 1-3, 3-2; Dundee United 3-1, 0-2; Dundee 2-0, 2-0.

Quarter-final: Morton 3-0, 3-1.

Semi-final: St Johnstone 4-0.

Final: bt Kilmarnock 1-0.

1963-64: Qualifying round: Falkirk 6-2, 3-0; Motherwell 0-3, 0-0; Partick Thistle 2-2, 2-2.

1964-65: Qualifying round: Kilmarnock 1-1, 0-1; Celtic 0-3, 1-6; Partick Thistle 1-2, 4-3.

1965-66: Qualifying round: Rangers 4-2, 0-1; Aberdeen 1-1, 2-0; Clyde 1-2, 2-1.

1966-67: Qualifying round: Celtic 0-2, 0-3; St Mirren 0-0, 3-1; Clyde 4-3, 3-1.

1967-68: Qualifying round: St Johnstone 1-2, 2-3; Stirling Albion 1-0, 4-1; Falkirk 2-0, 3-1.

1968-69: Qualifying round: Airdrie 3-2, 0-2; Dundee 2-1, 0-4; Kilmarnock 3-3, 0-0.

1969-70: Qualifying round: Dundee United 3-2, 1-0; St Mirren 0-0, 0-1; Morton 0-1, 2-0.

1970-71: Qualifying round: Celtic 1-2, 2-4; Dundee United 1-2, 0-0; Clyde 1-2, 5-1.

1971-72: Qualifying round: St Johnstone 4-1, 0-1; Airdrie 3-1, 1-2;Dunfermline 0-1, 4-0.

1972-73: Qualifying round: Dumbarton 0-1, 1-1; Airdrie 0-0, 1-2; Berwick Rangers 1-1, 3-0.

1973-74: Qualifying round: Partick Thistle 2-0, 0-0; St Johnstone 1-2, 4-1; Dundee 1-2, 0-0.

1974-75: Qualifying round: Aberdeen 1-0, 2-1; Dunfermline 2-3, 1-2; Morton 5-0, 2-0.
Quarter-final: Falkirk 0-0, 0-1.

1975-76: Qualifying round: Dumbarton 1-2, 6-0; Celtic 2-0, 1-3; Aberdeen 2-1, 1-0.

1976-77: Qualifying round: Dundee 2-0, 2-3; Partick Thistle 2-0, 3-3; Motherwell 2-1, 4-1.
Quarter-final: Falkirk 4-1, 3-4.
Semi-final: Celtic 1-2.

1977-78: First round: Stenhousemuir 1-0, 5-0.
Second round: Morton 3-0, 0-2.
Quarter-final: Dundee United 1-3, 2-0 (won 4-3 on penalties).
Semi-final: Celtic 0-2.

1978-79: First round: Morton 1-3, 1-4.

1979-80: First round: Ayr United 2-2, 0-1.

1980-81: First round: Montrose 2-1, 3-1.
Second round: Ayr United 2-3, 0-4.
1981-82: Qualifying round: Airdrie 1-0, 2-3; Aberdeen 1-0, 0-3; Kilmarnock 1-1, 0-2.

1982-83: Qualifying round: Motherwell 1-2, 1-0; Forfar 2-1, 2-0; Clyde 7-1, 3-0.
Quarter-final: St Mirren 1-1, 2-1.
Semi-final: Rangers 0-2, 1-2.

1983-84: Second round: Cowdenbeath 0-0, 1-1 (won 4-2 on penalties).
Third round: St Mirren 2-2, 3-1; Rangers 0-3, 0-2; Clydebank 1-1, 3-0.

1984-85: Second round: East Stirling 4-0.
Third round: Ayr United 1-0.
Quarter-final: Dundee 1-0.
Semi-final: Dundee United 1-2, 1-3.

1985-86: Second round: Montrose 3-1.
Third round: Stirling Albion 2-1.
Quarter-final: Aberdeen 0-1.

1986-87: Second round: Montrose 0-2.

1987-88: Second round: Kilmarnock 6-1.
Third round: Clyde 2-0.
Quarter-final: Rangers 1-4.

1988-89: Second round: St Johnstone 5-0.
Third round: Meadowbank Thistle 2-0.
Quarter-final: Dunfermline 4-1.
Semi-final: Rangers 0-3.

1989-90: Second round: Montrose 3-0.
Third round: Falkirk 4-1.
Quarter-final: Celtic 2-2 (lost 1-3 on penalties).

1990-91: Second round: Cowdenbeath 2-0.
Third round: St Mirren 1-0.
Quarter-final: Aberdeen 0-3.

1991-92: Second round: Clydebank 3-0.
Third round: Hamilton 2-0.
Quarter-final: Rangers 0-1.

1992-93: Second round: Clydebank 1-0.
Third round: Brechin City 2-1.
Quarter-final: Celtic 1-2.

1993-94: Second round: Stranraer 2-0.
Third round: Falkirk 0-1.

1994-95: Second round: Dumbarton 4-0.
Third round: St Johnstone 2-4.

1995-96: Second round: Alloa 3-0.
Third round: Dunfermline 2-1.
Quarter-final: Dundee 4-4 (lost 4-5 on penalties).

1996-97: Second round: Stenhousemuir 1-1 (won 5-4 on penalties).

Third round: St Johnstone 3-1.

Quarter-final: Celtic 1-0.

Semi-final: Dundee 3-1.

Final: lost 4-3 Rangers.

1997-98: Second round: Livingston 2-0.

Third round: Raith Rovers 2-1.

Quarter-final: Dunfermline 0-1.

League progress:

Season	Pld	Won	Lost	Drawn	For	Agnst	Pts	Postn
1890-91	18	6	10	2	31	37	14	6
1891-92	22	15	3	4	64	36	34	3
1892-93	18	8	8	2	39	42	18	4
1893-94	18	11	3	4	46	32	26	2
1894-95	18	15	2	1	50	18	31	1
1895-96	18	11	7	0	68	35	22	4
1896-97	18	13	3	2	47	22	28	1
1897-98	18	8	6	4	54	33	20	4
1898-99	18	12	4	2	56	30	26	2
1899-1900	18	10	5	3	41	24	23	4
1900-01	20	5	11	4	22	30	14	10
1901-02	18	10	6	2	32	21	22	3
1902-03	22	11	5	6	46	27	28	4
1903-04	26	18	5	3	63	35	39	2
1904-05	26	11	12	3	46	44	25	7
1905-06	30	18	5	7	64	27	43	2
1906-07	34	11	10	13	46	43	35	9
1907-08	34	11	17	6	50	22	28	11
1908-09	34	12	14	8	54	49	32	11
1909-10	34	12	15	7	59	50	31	11
1910-11	34	8	18	8	42	59	24	14
1911-12	34	16	10	8	54	40	40	4
1912-13	34	17	10	7	71	43	41	3
1913-14	38	23	7	8	70	29	54	3
1914-15	38	27	4	7	83	32	61	2
1915-16*	37	20	11	6	66	45	46	5
1916-17	38	14	20	4	44	59	32	14
1917-18	34	14	16	4	41	58	32	10
1918-19	34	14	11	9	59	52	37	7
1919-20	42	14	19	9	57	72	37	15
1920-21	42	20	12	10	74	49	50	3
1921-22	42	11	21	10	50	60	32	19
1922-23	38	11	12	15	51	50	37	11
1923-24	38	14	14	10	61	50	38	9
1924-25	38	12	15	11	65	69	35	10
1925-26	38	21	9	8	87	56	50	3

Season	Pld	Won	Lost	Drawn	For	Agnst	Pts	Postn
1926-27	38	12	15	11	65	64	35	13
1927-28	38	20	11	7	89	50	47	4
1928-29	38	19	10	9	91	57	47	4
1929-30	38	14	15	9	69	69	37	10
1930-31	38	19	13	6	90	63	44	5
1931-32	38	17	16	5	63	61	39	8
1932-33	38	21	9	8	84	51	50	3
1933-34	38	17	11	10	86	59	44	6
1934-35	38	20	8	10	87	52	50	3
1935-36	38	20	11	7	88	55	47	5
1936-37	38	24	11	3	99	60	51	5
1937-38	38	26	6	6	90	50	58	2
1938-39	38	20	13	5	98	70	45	4
1939-40*x	29	18	7	4	104	66	40	2
1940-41y	30	12	13	5	64	71	29	10
1941-42y	30	14	12	4	85	72	32	5
1942-43y	30	12	11	7	68	64	31	7
1943-44y	30	14	9	7	67	50	35	4
1944-45y	30	14	9	7	75	60	35	5
1945-46	30	11	11	8	63	57	30	7
1946-47	30	16	8	6	52	43	38	4
1947-48	30	10	12	8	37	42	28	9
1948-49	30	12	12	6	64	54	30	8
1949-50	30	20	7	3	86	40	43	3
1950-51	30	16	9	5	72	45	37	4
1951-52	30	14	9	7	69	53	35	4
1952-53	30	12	12	6	59	50	30	4
1953-54	30	16	8	6	70	45	38	2
1954-55	30	16	7	7	74	45	39	4
1955-56	34	19	8	7	99	47	45	3
1956-57	34	24	5	5	81	48	53	2
1957-58	34	29	1	4	132	29	62	1
1958-59	34	21	7	6	92	51	48	2
1959-60	34	23	3	8	102	51	54	1
1960-61	34	13	13	8	51	53	34	8
1961-62	34	16	12	6	54	49	38	6
1962-63	34	17	8	2	85	59	43	5
1963-64	34	19	6	9	74	40	47	4

Season	Pld	Won	Lost	Drawn	For	Agnst	Pts	Postn
1964-65	34	22	6	6	90	49	50	2
1965-66	34	13	9	12	56	48	38	7
1966-67	34	11	15	8	39	48	30	11
1967-68	34	13	17	4	56	61	30	12
1968-69	34	14	12	8	52	64	36	8
1969-70	34	13	9	12	50	36	38	4
1970-71	34	13	14	7	41	40	33	11
1971-72	34	13	8	13	53	49	39	6
1972-73	34	12	16	6	39	50	30	10
1973-74	34	14	10	10	54	43	38	6
1974-75	34	11	10	13	47	52	35	8
1975-76	36	13	14	9	39	45	39	5
1976-77	36	7	16	13	49	66	27	9
1977-78	39	24	5	10	77	42	58	2
1978-79	36	8	21	7	39	71	23	9
1979-80	39	20	6	13	58	39	53	1
1980-81	36	6	24	6	27	71	18	10
1981-82	39	21	10	8	65	37	50	3
1982-83	39	22	7	10	79	38	54	2
1983-84	36	10	10	16	38	47	36	5
1984-85	36	13	18	5	47	64	31	7
1985-86	36	20	6	10	59	33	50	2
1986-87	44	21	9	13	64	43	55	5
1987-88	44	23	5	16	74	32	62	2
1988-89	36	9	14	13	35	42	31	6
1989-90	36	16	8	12	54	35	44	3
1990-91	36	14	15	7	48	55	35	5
1991-92	44	27	8	9	60	37	63	2
1992-93	44	15	15	14	46	51	44	5
1993-94	44	11	13	20	37	43	42	7
1994-95	36	12	17	7	44	51	43	6
1995-96	36	16	13	7	55	53	55	4
1996-97	36	14	12	10	46	43	52	4
1997-98	36	19	7	10	70	46	64	3

*incomplete programme, x Scottish Regional League, y Scottish Southern League.

European record:

1958-59: European Cup: First round: Standard Liege (Belgium) 1-5 (a) 2-1 (h).

1960-61: European Cup: First round: Benfica (Portugal) 1-2 (h), 0-3 (a).

1961-62: Fairs Cup: First round: Union St Gilloise (Luxembourg) 3-1 (a), 2-0 (h).

Second round: Inter Milan (Italy) 0-1 (h), 0-4 (a).

1963-64: Fairs Cup: First round: Lausanne (Switzerland) 2-2 (a), 2-2 (h),2-3 (play-off).

1965-66: Fairs Cup: Second round: Valerengens (Norway) 1-0 (h), 3-1 (a).

Third round: Zarragoza (Spain) 3-3 (h), 2-2 (a), 0-1 (play-off).

1976-77: Cup-Winners' Cup: First round: Locomotiv Leipzig (Germany) 0-2 (a), 5-1 (h).

Second round: Hamburg (Germany) 2-4 (a), 1-4 (h).

1984-85: UEFA Cup: First round: Paris St Germain (France) 0-4 (a), 2-2 (h).

1986-87: UEFA Cup: First round: Dukla Prague (Czech Rep) 3-2 (h), 0-1 (a).

1988-89: UEFA Cup: First round: St Patrick's (Ireland) 2-0 (a), 2-0 (h).

Second round: Austria Vienna (Austria) 0-0 (h), 1-0 (a).

Third round: Velez Mostar (Bosnia) 3-0 (h), 1-2 (a).

Quarter-final: Bayern Munich (Germany) 1-0 (h), 0-2 (a).

1990-91: UEFA Cup: First round: Dnepr (Ukraine) 1-1 (a), 3-1 (h).

Second round: Bologna (Italy) 3-1 (h), 0-3 (a).

1992-93: UEFA Cup: First round: Slavia Prague (Czech Rep) 0-1 (a), 4-2 (h).

Second round: FC Liege (Belgium) 0-1 (h), 0-1 (a).

1993-94: UEFA Cup: First round: Atletico Madrid (Spain) 2-1 (h), 0-3 (a).

1996-97: Cup-Winners' Cup: Preliminary round: Red Star Belgrade

(Yugoslavia) 0-0 (a), 1-1 (h).